WHY JURY DUTY
MATTERS

WHY JURY DUTY
MATTERS

A CITIZEN'S GUIDE TO CONSTITUTIONAL ACTION

ANDREW GUTHRIE FERGUSON

WITH A FOREWORD BY CHARLES J. OGLETREE JR.

NEW YORK UNIVERSITY PRESS
New York and London

NEW YORK UNIVERSITY PRESS
New York and London
www.nyupress.org

References to Internet websites (URLs) were accurate
at the time of writing. Neither the author nor New York University
Press is responsible for URLs that may have expired or changed
since the manuscript was prepared.

LIBRARY OF CONGRESS CATALOGING-IN-PUBLICATION DATA
Ferguson, Andrew G.
Why jury duty matters : a citizen's guide to constitutional action / Andrew Guthrie
Ferguson ; with a foreword by Charles Ogletree Jr.
p. cm.
Includes bibliographical references and index.
ISBN 978-0-8147-2902-1 (cl : alk. paper)
ISBN 978-0-8147-2903-8 (pb : alk. paper)
ISBN 978-0-8147-2904-5 (ebook)
ISBN 978-0-8147-2905-2 (ebook)
1. Jury duty—United States. I. Title.
KF8972.F47 2012
347.73'752—dc23   2012024879

New York University Press books are printed on acid-free paper,
and their binding materials are chosen for strength and durability.
We strive to use environmentally responsible suppliers and materials
to the greatest extent possible in publishing our books.

Manufactured in the United States of America
10 9 8 7 6 5 4 3 2 1

*This book is dedicated to the millions of citizens
who serve our courts.
Your presence is a daily inspiration
to the system of justice.*

CONTENTS

ACKNOWLEDGMENTS

I owe a great debt to my family, Alissa, Cole, Mom and Dad, Anndrea, Michael, Ann, and Tom for reading and commenting on drafts of this book and giving me love, confidence, and the education to make my ideas a reality.

I wish to thank my colleagues at the Public Defender Service for the District of Columbia for their inspiration and dedication to their clients and the courts. I also wish to thank my counterparts at the United States Attorney's Office for their respect and collegiality. Many judges from the District of Columbia Superior Court took the time to review this book and provide helpful comments. I want to thank them for teaching me about the jury system. In addition, Professors Neil Vidmar, Nancy Marder, Charles J. Ogletree Jr., and David Rudovsky, Judges Gregory Mize and William C. Pryor, and others have given their positive feedback to improve this book.

I wish to thank my faculty colleagues and students at the David A. Clarke School of Law at the University of the District of Columbia for their support and kindness, and most especially Dean Shelley Broderick for her faith and assistance in making this project a reality.

To those jurors who unknowingly inspired this book and provided the source material, I owe a debt of gratitude. Your stories and our conversations are etched in my heart (if not in my notes), as I did not record them verbatim. All errors in memory are mine alone.

There are many wonderful organizations devoted to constitutional understanding, civic literacy, and the jury. For this book, I wish to mention the Federal Judicial Center, which provided a wonderful wealth of archival photographs of historic courthouses on their History of the Federal Judiciary website. The National Center for State Courts has done a fabulous job collecting data on jury service in the United States. The National Archives in Washington and the National Constitution Center in Philadelphia have served as personal points of constitutional inspiration (and should be visited by every American at some point during their lives). The American Bar Association and the local bar associations have devoted much effort to inspire citizens to care about jury service. Each one of these organizations has extensive informational resources for citizens interested in the courts, the Constitution, or the institution of the jury.

Finally, I would like to thank my editor, Deborah Gershenowitz, and NYU Press for seeing the value of this work of public scholarship.

FOREWORD

The American Jury System: Democracy at Work

A jury verdict changed my life. It was 1972. I was in college at Stanford University and the trial was about a half hour away in San Jose. I was a part of a large group of African American students at Stanford University who had been organizing against the criminal prosecution of Angela Davis. Davis—a political prisoner, black activist, and alleged criminal—had been charged with aiding the kidnapping and murder of a judge during the attempted escape of several prisoners from a criminal courtroom. The Angela Davis trial, mixing murder with racial politics, was one of the most controversial legal spectacles of the early 1970s. Our task was not simple. Ronald Reagan was the Governor of California and Richard Nixon was the President. Our solution would not be a political one, but rather putting faith in the twelve people who would decide Angela Davis's guilt or innocence. Personally convinced of her innocence,

I and other students had organized to protest what we saw as another unfair target of the criminal justice system, and what we assumed would be a politically motivated conviction.[1] How could the face of black radical politics get a fair trial before an all-white jury?

On the day of the verdict, we pensively awaited the jury's decision. In a California courtroom, seven men and five women defied a history of racial injustice and our expectations. The "not guilty" verdict provided a full and surprising vindication. It was a public trial. It was an impartial jury. Davis had the benefit of competent and committed defense lawyers. They were, in my view, the original "Dream Team," led by four progressives: Howard Moore, Leo Branton, Doris Walker, and a close childhood friend of Professor Davis, Margaret Burnham. Yet it was still a revelation that the system of justice worked. Through the Angela Davis trial, I became aware of the critical role that lawyers, judges, and juries can and should play in securing justice. From that moment on, I knew I wanted to pursue a career in the law. It was the first murder trial I ever witnessed, but it would not be the last.

In 1978 I entered the legal profession as a public defender. In short order, I regularly appeared before criminal juries in the District of Columbia Superior Court. Standing before twelve citizens and standing up for one accused defendant were among the most humbling and formative experiences of my professional life. As a trial lawyer, each client, each case, and each jury was different. I learned that jurors have a wide range of life experiences that help provide them with the insight to fairly assess the particular facts of each case. I represented the young and old, men and women, black, brown, and white, and so many others. I represented those presumed guilty, the truly innocent, and, again, everyone in between. And it all happened in front of a jury.

During those early years, I saw juries struggle with the power being entrusted to them day after day. Just as you develop a compelling narrative in a closing argument, you develop a relationship with a jury. In murder cases or other serious criminal cases, the emotional bond between lawyer and jury becomes palpable. I envisioned my advocacy reaching across the wooden railing of the jury box and into the thoughts, and then the deliberations, of the jurors. I do not know if it worked, but I do know that the juries worked hard at their jobs. In the trenches of criminal court, it is hard not to be impressed with the jury.

Yet I was not unmindful of my role as a Harvard-educated lawyer, arguing before predominantly African American juries, for almost exclusively African American clients. My success for my clients was not typical of the history of racially segregated and racially biased juries in the United States. Unlike many jurisdictions, the District of Columbia had racially balanced jury panels and, in my view, the best public defender agency in the country. Hard work, intelligence, and more hard work could get positive results. However, as a busy trial lawyer I did not have the luxury to ponder the historical or systemic inequities of the jury system. All one could do is hope that the twelve citizens before me would do the right thing, listen to my argument, and take seriously the life and liberty of my client.

As a law professor at Harvard, I have spent a career training a generation of legal advocates in criminal law and procedure and its historical context. The history of racial inequality in juries is not only depressing, but also often deadly. Innocent men and women, many of color, have been convicted unjustly by all-white juries. Equally troubling, history reminds us in cases like that of the individuals prosecuted for the murder of Emmett Till in 1955, factually guilty white men and women have been acquitted by similarly constituted juries because racial discrimination, not law, controlled the outcome. The line between due process and lynch mob was not always so clear.[2] Further, the United States has seen formal and informal barriers to racially inclusive jury selection processes. Legal, social, and bureaucratic roadblocks to diversity have been erected and dismantled, and then erected again. The evolution has been forward moving, but it is never complete. Even in this new century, charges of racial discrimination in jury selection and jury venires are being litigated. Large segments of communities—mostly those of color—continue to be excluded. We have made great progress, but there is much progress to be made.

This book identifies how you, as a juror, can continue that progress. Central to every trial—be it on behalf of a powerless prisoner or a powerful politician—is the jury. Like American democracy itself, the jury represents the best ideals of this country. Both democratic citizenship and jury service require participation, deliberation, a respect for equality, fairness, dissent, and most importantly, a fundamental faith in individual liberty. To witness jury service at its best is to see the United States at its best. It must be inclusive, open, and representative of the diversity of the country.

The constitutional values discussed in this book—equality, liberty, participation, fairness, dissent, accountability, the common good—were values that motivated me to become a lawyer. They sustain my teaching. They are the values of the civil rights movement because they are the values of the United States. Charles Hamilton Houston, perhaps America's greatest civil rights genius of all time, was a DC native, graduate of Harvard Law School, and teacher at Howard Law School, who won his first Supreme Court victory for the NAACP by appealing a criminal conviction from a segregated, unequal jury.[3] As a Supreme Court Justice, Thurgood Marshall wrote about the harm of excluding segments of society. In *Peters v. Kiff*, he stated, "Illegal and unconstitutional jury selection procedures cast doubt on the integrity of the whole judicial process. They create the appearance of bias in the decision of individual cases, and they increase the risk of actual bias as well."[4] To preserve the legitimacy of the legal system, all citizens had to participate. Having persons of color on the jury provided a measure of accountability for crimes against minorities, just as much as it ensured a sense of fairness for the defendant or integrity to the system of justice. Participation in jury service for all people was, thus, a central victory in the battle for civil rights. In a criminal case marking the beginning of the Supreme Court's refusal to tolerate discrimination against minority jurors, Thurgood Marshall supported the Supreme Court's decision to end the racial use of peremptory challenges against jurors. In many senses prescient, Justice Marshall advocated to end the use of peremptory challenges altogether.[5]

Today, perhaps as a measure of our progress, all races and all citizens groan equally loudly when the jury summons arrives in the mail. Today, the right to participate occasionally becomes overshadowed with the obligations and inconvenience attendant to the summons. Yet the reason why participation in jury service matters has not changed over the years. The constitutional strength of this country begins with its citizens.

A jury gives ordinary people extraordinary power. It is a constitutional power. And sadly, it is a not always a recognized and appreciated power.

This book begins where I began as a lawyer, in the hallways of the Superior Court of the District of Columbia. Written by a public defender, now law professor, it reflects on the constitutional values that define our national identity and our legal system. It asks that as citizens we take our obligation as jurors seriously. It asks that we see the potential of the jury system and our responsibility to make the system work.

It was a similar hope that led me to follow the trial of Angela Davis in that California courtroom decades ago and to become a defense lawyer. We attended the trial with the hope that justice could be done by thoughtful, engaged citizens summoned to participate in our constitutional system. That day, like every day in courtrooms all across the United States, the jury system worked.

At the end of the Angela Davis trial, the presiding judge, Richard E. Arnason, excused the jury with the following words.[6] Quoting from G. K. Chesterton's observation of the jury process almost a century ago, Judge Arnason read:

> Our civilization has decided, and very justly decided, that determining the guilt or innocence of men is a thing too important to be trusted to trained men. It wishes for light upon that awful matter, it asks men who know no more law than I know, but who can feel the things I felt in the jury box. When it wants a library catalogued, or the solar system discovered, or any trifle of that kind, it uses up its specialists. But when it wishes anything done which is really serious, it collects twelve of the ordinary

men standing round. The same thing was done, if I remember right, by the founder of Christianity.[7]

It is true today, as it was then. The jury's strength—legal, constitutional, moral—rests with ordinary Americans like you. It is the very essence of our democracy.

CHARLES J. OGLETREE JR., HARVARD UNIVERSITY

The Constitution is all that gives us a national character.
—Daniel Webster

City Hall (n.d., ca. 1916) Completed in 1849 (third phase)
ARCHITECT: George Hadfield
The Circuit Court of the District of Columbia met here from 1823 until
that court was abolished in 1863; the Supreme Court of the District of
Columbia met here from 1863 until 1936; the District Court of the United
States for the District of Columbia met here from 1936 until 1948; the
United States District Court for the District of Columbia met here from
1948 until 1952; the Court of Appeals for the District of Columbia met
here from 1893 until 1910. Now in use by local government.

INTRODUCTION

In a poorly lit hallway, on an uncomfortable bench, a young man sits wringing his hands. Around him hums the bustle of an urban courthouse. Uniformed police officers, slick-suited lawyers, and casually dressed witnesses go in and out of the courtroom doors. Were he paying close attention, the young man could witness the anguished aftermath of a murder sentencing or a messy divorce down the hall.

But at that moment, the man is concentrating on himself. Or perhaps, more specifically, the man is concentrating on twelve jurors behind a closed door—twelve jurors deliberating his fate. The man has just witnessed a trial—his own. He has seen due process of law firsthand. He faces accountability and the stark choice of incarceration or liberty. A choice that now belongs to the jurors in his case.

Inside that jury room, twelve citizens sit around a wooden table. They share little in common save for the jury badges affixed to their chests. Despite different backgrounds, they face one another as equals, each person given no more power than anyone else. No matter their position in society, in that jury room they have but one vote. And vote they must. They have been asked to participate in a fundamentally American process—the deliberation of guilt or innocence in a criminal trial. They have just experienced a legal process that they hope was fair and just. Today is their day of decision.

As a public defender practicing in an urban courthouse, I have sat on that uncomfortable bench with my clients many times. And occasionally, during those nervous waits, I turn to the document that brought me there—the United States Constitution. In the copy I carry, the print is small and the words old-fashioned. Yet that single document influences everything that is happening in the courthouse. I watch as constitutional ideals such as civic participation, deliberation, fairness, equality, liberty, accountability, freedom of conscience, and the common good come alive through the practice of ordinary citizens. I witness jurors applying constitutional principles to reach a fair verdict. I wonder if they know their closeness to the Constitution.

* * *

This book began on that courthouse bench, observing constitutional values in action. It was written with the realization that most of us—my client, the litigants, the witnesses, and most especially the jurors—do not see the constitutional principles all around us. These good citizens are playing a role at the heart of our constitutional structure without realizing their connection to the larger principles of our nation.

This is not to say that citizens do not value the Constitution. To the contrary, the United States Constitution remains our most sacred national document. Most citizens would lay down their lives to preserve it. Yet, despite an abstract faith in the Constitution, we remain disconnected from its practice. Most decent and well-meaning citizens haven't read the text of the Constitution since high school (if then). Many otherwise conscientious Americans remain constitutionally uninformed, knowing more about current television contests than current legal decisions.[1] And while we might read about the latest hot-button issue ending up before the Supreme Court, only a handful of us ever have a direct connection with a legal issue, much less a constitutional court case.

Yet the truth is that we are all constitutional actors. As a citizen—regardless of whether you want to accept it—you have been entrusted to act within the constitutional system.

This book seeks to reconnect you to those constitutional principles through one of the last unifying acts of citizenship—jury duty. Yes, jury duty—our recurring civic obligation to head down to the courthouse and participate in resolving a criminal or civil case involving members of the community. It is an important but usually much dreaded task. It presents a necessary but inconvenient moment of civic responsibility. A sad reality, really, as jury trials were notably at the forefront of our established constitutional rights.

The premise of this book is simple: imagine that instead of considering jury duty an inconvenience, you considered it a day of reflection—a day to reevaluate your role as a constitutional actor. After all, a jury summons provides a government-provided free pass from your normal family and work responsibilities. It is literally the law of the land that you cannot complete your everyday routine. Jury duty thus provides an opportunity (with plenty of waiting time) to reflect on our constitutional values. In addition, you have the chance to practice the constitutional principles that have served this country well.

Why care about constitutional principles? The United States Constitution exists as the repository of our national ideals. We are "Americans" because of ideals, not ethnicity, religion, or culture. Remember, we live in a country where it is permissible to salute the flag or burn it as a constitutional expression of the First Amendment's right to free speech.[2] In the name of being American, you can accept or reject the symbols of America.

But the insight of the Founders was not simply to put our ideals down on paper, but to create mechanisms to practice those ideals. The Constitution provides a framework not only for government, but also for civic and political engagement. The jury is but one of the institutional structures designed to turn ideals into reality. You might believe in fairness and accountability, but as a juror you get to apply those principles to the young man sitting twenty feet from you at the defendant's table. As a juror you are forced to translate ideals into action. In many ways, that is the hope of this book—to translate shared constitutional principles into daily practice in an effort to strengthen our nation's constitutional character.

Why jury duty? The fact is that jury duty is one of the few constitutional rights that every American has the opportunity to experience. It remains an American civic ritual. It connects people across class, national origin, religion, gender, and race. It creates habits of focus and purpose, and teaches values necessary for democracy. No matter your education level or importance, you share this constitutional right and obligation. And, truth be told, as a trial lawyer who relied on criminal juries for the liberty of my clients, I can think of no institution more deserving of a sustained project of reflection and respect.

Equally important, juries were foundational to America. It is no overstatement to say that those who created this nation ranked the right to trial by jury as the greatest source of liberty.[3] A jury trial was guaranteed in the Charter that founded the first English settlement at Jamestown in 1607.[4] The lack of jury trials was an explicit grievance listed by Thomas Jefferson in the Declaration of Independence—"depriving us in many cases, of the benefit of trial by jury"[5]—a complaint that helped spark the American Revolution. Between the Declaration of Independence in 1776 and the signing of the Constitution in 1787, each of the colonies established the constitutional right to a criminal jury trial for its citizens.[6]

At the founding of the United States, the right to a jury trial was one of the first constitutional rights agreed to at the Constitutional Convention in Philadelphia.[7] And it is the *only* right that appears in both the text of the Constitution and the Bill of Rights.[8] In the Bill of Rights, three of the first ten Amendments expressly protect juries. The Fifth Amendment protects the grand jury, the Sixth Amendment protects the criminal jury, and the Seventh Amendment protects the civil jury.[9] Further, at the time of the drafting of the Constitution, both the First Amendment protection from prior restraint of speech[10] and the Fourth Amendment's protection from unreasonable searches and seizures[11] were effectuated by civil jury trials—meaning *that half* of the Bill of Rights was, in one way or another, focused on the right to a trial by jury.[12] In fact, the right to a jury was one of the only things all the Founding Fathers could agree on. As Alexander Hamilton wrote in *Federalist No. 83*:

> The friends and adversaries of the plan of the [Constitutional] convention, if they agree in nothing else, concur at least in the value they set upon the trial by jury: Or if there is any difference between them, it consists in this; the former regard it as a valuable

safeguard to liberty, the latter represent it as the very palladium of free government.[13]

From this historical foundation, jury trials have remained at the center of our American justice system. There are approximately 150,000 jury trials a year with more than 1.5 million actual sitting jurors.[14] Almost 32 million of your fellow citizens receive a jury summons.[15] One in three Americans will serve on a jury in their lifetime.[16] The American Bar Association has determined that 78 percent of the public rates the jury system as the fairest method to determine guilt or innocence in a criminal case, and 69 percent consider juries to be the most important part of our justice system.[17] It is an American practice, crafted around our common law tradition and incorporating our fundamental values. The result is that the United States currently holds 90 percent of the world's criminal jury trials and almost all of its civil jury trials.[18]

Moreover, even though the history of the jury (in actual practice) has not always lived up to its stated ideals, the modern jury stands as success story, remaining consistent with our constitutional standards of fairness and inclusion. We have moved past the ugly history of direct racial and gender discrimination,[19] as well as "blue ribbon" or "key-man"[20] jury systems that invariably selected only "qualified" jurors and excluded people of color and women.[21] State by state, the rule of law has been systematized so it applies fairly across courtrooms and the nation.

Today's jury should be celebrated. As currently constituted, the jury is an institution that connects local farm towns and urban metropolises. It strives for fairness and equality. It remains localized and democratic. It has developed into a model for how we should behave as citizens. Jury experience exists as one of the remaining connecting threads in a wonderfully diverse United States. It links us to our founding principles and challenges us to live up to them.

Each chapter in this book takes a constitutionally grounded principle and shows how it applies in jury duty. The principles discussed here represent an incomplete and probably contestable list of core constitutional values. Legal scholars may debate the original intent of the Founders, parsing textual fragments and citing ancient cases, but there is little question that "liberty," "due process of law," "accountable government," and "participation" were considered fundamental values. Whatever your political background or legal views, recognizing the ideals of "equality," "freedom of conscience," or "deliberation" as essential to the national character allows you to appreciate constitutional values without choosing political sides. Jury service is apolitical, as should be a solid grounding in American constitutional history and text.

Of course, the constitutional principles discussed in this book extend beyond jury service. This is but an introduction to the Constitution and the value and values of jury duty. I encourage you to go beyond this brief beginning to understand both the foresight of our Founding Fathers and the history of the United States Constitution. This book has a simple goal: to reconnect each of us with this important document and reclaim a sense of constitutional character while on jury duty.

The jury system postulates a conscious duty of participation in the machinery of justice. . . . One of its greatest benefits is in the security it gives the people that they, as jurors actual or possible, being part of the judicial system of the country can prevent its arbitrary use or abuse.

—Chief Justice William Howard Taft

U.S. Courthouse (1900, 1938) Completed in 1882
SUPERVISING ARCHITECTS: William Appleton Potter and James G. Hill
Extension completed in 1938
SUPERVISING ARCHITECT OF EXTENSION: Louis A. Simon
The United States District Court for the Middle District of Tennessee met here until 1952; the United States Circuit Court for the Middle District of Tennessee met here until that court was abolished in 1912. Now owned by the city.

SOURCE: UNITED STATES TREASURY DEPARTMENT, *A HISTORY OF PUBLIC BUILDINGS* (WASHINGTON, DC: GPO, 1901), 556–57.

1

An Invitation to Participation

A Summons

The letter arrives in the mail. "Dear Citizen" it begins.

You hold in your hand an invitation. Sure, it looks like an official jury summons, and it was probably not the invitation you were hoping to receive. Yet it is still an invitation—an invitation to participate in the American experiment of self-government.

It is not every day that we get an invitation saying "come join your extended neighborhood—meet the postal worker, cafeteria chef, banker, professor, or truck driver down the block." It is not often that you are asked to socialize with a randomly selected group comprising all the types of people who live in your city or town. And you can feel flattered that you have been invited. It means that you have not committed a felony[1] (that anyone knows about), that you are mature enough to judge others,[2] and that your community needs you. Of course, it might be

9

nicer if your "invitation" was gold-embossed with fancy lettering, rather than the dot-matrix copy that remains in some courthouses, but whatever the paper stock or font, it is an invitation that millions of Americans receive every year.[3] And it's only polite to accept.

As you ponder the conflicts that the jury date poses with your schedule—work deadlines, family vacations, day care, and the like—remember that you have been invited in a role independent of those responsibilities. You were invited because you are a citizen, not a mother, father, daughter, employee, boss, or unemployed actor. Nothing you have accomplished or failed to accomplish is relevant to your service. The summons requires you to consider yourself in a new role distinct from the identity you have spent your life creating. The famous and not famous appear before the court in the same position. Even judges when called to jury duty in their own courthouses have no more power than does the ordinary layperson. You are simply a citizen—a citizen with an important responsibility.

That responsibility is usually mixed with a bit of uncertainty. Uncertainty about the process. Uncertainty about the time commitment. Uncertainty about the expectations.[4] This uncertainty is to be expected. There is an information imbalance in the irregular requirement of jury service. You have been asked to play a role in the justice system, but what role, for how long, and about what subject has not yet been decided. You might end up a jury foreperson in a scandalous civil trial, or an alternate in a petty criminal case, or never selected after hours of waiting in the jurors' lounge. While uncertainty abounds, it is a responsibility that requires your physical presence. You have to get up, head to the courthouse, and see what happens.

A jury summons is an invitation to participation. Jurors are asked to involve themselves in some of the most personal, sensational, and terrifying events in a community. It is real life, usually real tragedy, played out in court. Jurors confront disturbing facts, bloody images, or heart-wrenching testimony.[5] There is no way to hide when one is shown the blown-up, blue-tinged autopsy photograph of a dead man, or the results of some horrible accident involving a defective product. A jury may have to decide whether a man lives or dies, or whether a multimillion-dollar company goes bankrupt. A jury will have to pass judgment in a way that will have real-world effects on the parties before the court.

Of course, before you get to the heightened emotion of trial, your participation may feel more like a trip to the local Department of Motor Vehicles—a lot of bureaucratic waiting, punctuated by seemingly inefficient systems for organizing the mass of people who arrive each day. Actually, it's a pretty efficient process in most courthouses, but for the uninitiated, it might not seem that way.

As you wait, look around the jurors' lounge and observe the diversity of your fellow citizens. Almost every shape, form, and type of American sits around you. Some sit around discomforted by the waiting and frustration. Others seem to be looking forward to the opportunity to stay and serve. People are reading history books and comic books, people are knitting sweaters and writing computer code, people from all walks of life sit together, expecting to become a part of something (or hoping to avoid it).

Of course, whether viewed positively or negatively, your jury summons is not optional. You can't respectfully decline attendance at this year's criminal or civil trial. In some jurisdictions, United States Marshals are sent to haul jury duty scofflaws into court to face contempt proceedings.[6] Both the skipping of jury service and the punishment are ancient traditions. In colonial Virginia, absent jurors were fined in pounds of tobacco for their failure to attend as requested.[7] Today, you might be looking at a \$500 penalty.[8]

So, holding that summons skeptically, one question you might have is "why was I invited?" Odds are you are not a lawyer, constitutional scholar, or experienced judge, so why were you—unelected and untrained you—asked to participate in rendering judgment? As the esteemed Harvard Law School Dean Erwin Griswold commented, "Why should anyone think that 12 persons brought in from the street, selected in various ways, for their lack of general ability, should have any special capacity for deciding controversies between persons?"[9] And while overly cynical, it is, in part, true. No one in the United States is trained to become a juror. There are no classes, no crash courses, no study aids.[10] So why would you be asked to participate in something you have never been taught to do?

The answer goes to the heart of our constitutional system of government. The "We the People" that begins the Preamble to the Constitution means you:

> We the People of the United States . . . do ordain and establish this Constitution for the United States of America.[11]

We established a system of government in which "we the people" are sovereign. And sovereigns have to govern. We require people to participate in a government "of the people, by the people, and for the people."[12] Popular sovereignty (meaning the voting booth you see once every two to four years) ensures that the power comes from you—not a king, not a religious figure, but you—the same person shaking your head at that jury summons. As Justice Louis Brandeis once famously stated, "The only title in our democracy superior to that of President is the title of citizen."[13] In practical terms, this means you are summoned to participate in jury duty because you are the source of constitutional power.

The Jury

The jury evolved over centuries of continental and British experimentation before reaching American shores.[14] Yet the American jury during our Founding era was something quite unlike its forebears. Far more than merely a fact-finding body, colonial criminal juries acted as legal revolutionaries on occasion, defying British rule.

One of the great causes that captured the attention of the fledgling nation was the unfairness of the Stamp Act. You may remember from American history that the stamp taxes on tea and other goods became a symbolic rallying cry against British oppression, leading to the Boston Tea Party.[15] Yet the concern was not simply the taxes, but the fact that violators of the Act were to be tried in admiralty courts *without a jury*.[16] Colonial anger toward the Stamp Act included a jury demand. And it went further. Local criminal juries refused to enforce British customs laws[17] and prevented convictions for seditious libel against the British Crown.[18] Local civil juries even awarded damages for colonial smugglers caught circumventing British law.[19] In short, juries became an instrument of the struggle that resulted in revolutionary demands at the Stamp Act Congress of 1765, the First Continental Congress in 1774, and ultimately the Declaration of Independence in 1776—a declaration that listed King George's denial of "the benefit of trial by jury" as one of its justifications for independence and war.[20] The Tea Party was not just about taxes, but also about juries.

At the same time, colonial juries did manage to maintain some of the participatory practices of traditional fact-finding bodies. One of the more celebrated criminal trials of the time involved eight British soldiers who were accused of murdering several Boston citizens in 1770.[21] In what became known as the "Boston Massacre," these foreign soldiers had been accused of shooting into a mob of angry colonists. Paul Revere rallied Boston into a frenzy of anger and resentment over the death of five men, including Crispus Attucks.[22] The British were already despised in those prerevolutionary days, making a Boston jury a difficult forum for a fair trial. Yet the decision was made to keep the trial in Boston. As Akhil Amar wrote, "[P]atriots had insisted that fair trials could and should be held in Boston itself, in proceedings that would showcase both community rights *and* defendant rights, republican freedom *and* individual fairness."[23] Future President John Adams (then just a young lawyer) took the soldiers' unpopular case. Suffering community opprobrium, Adams successfully argued that the soldiers had acted in self-defense against the angry mob, asserting, "Facts are stubborn things . . . and whatever may be our wishes, our inclinations, or the dictums of our passions, they cannot alter the state of facts and evidence."[24] Asking the jury to consider how the soldiers should have acted facing the "rabble," throwing "rubbish" and yelling "Kill them! Kill them!" Adams managed to convince his fellow Massachusetts citizen–jurors to acquit six out of the eight soldiers and get lesser charges for the other two.[25] The exonerations gained an added legitimacy from the participation of the local community jury.[26]

From our perspective today, colonial juries, especially grand juries, were almost activist, exercising powers we would now consider properly handled by the other branches of government.[27] Grand jurors today weigh evidence on individual suspects in individual cases presented by prosecutors. Colonial grand juries, however, went so far as to be tasked with inspecting roads, monitoring public expenditures, investigating public corruption, and overseeing pauper laws and prisons.[28] In Virginia, courts relied on grand juries for advice on assessing taxes and the construction of public buildings.[29] Early Massachusetts grand juries were free to investigate *any* abuse of governmental power or use of funds.[30]

As a model of citizen-based self-government (or at least the portion of white male "citizens"), the drafters of the Constitution could not have done better than to follow the successful practice of juries. Jury participation, like voting participation, was deemed the best way to protect citizens from a larger central government:[31] "Just as suffrage ensures the people's ultimate control in the legislative and executive branches, jury trial is meant to ensure their control in the judiciary."[32] By immersing jurors in the actual administration of justice, they would be empowered to protect fellow citizens.

But where does this idea of citizen participation come from? The answer is that it comes from the Constitution itself.

Participation and the Constitution

Your presence as a juror is but one example of the constitutional requirement that citizens engage in government. A quick look through the constitutional text demonstrates an emphasis on citizen participation in other areas such as the right to vote, assemble, organize, and contribute to our democracy.

The Vote

Electoral participation—how we vote, who votes, when we vote—centers the constitutional design. Begin at the beginning. Article I sets forth the structure of the Legislative Branch—the Senate and the House of Representatives. Legislators elected by your vote.

Article I provides for the rules of elections, eligibility requirements, and the manner in which the legislature would be ordered. Specifically, Article I, Section 2, establishes the election of congressional representatives by the people every two years,

> *The House of Representatives shall be composed of Members chosen every second year by the people of the several states …*

These congressional representatives remain closest to the people, and they are elected directly by the people.

Although a little less direct, the original Article I, Section 3, established the election of Senators through state legislatures elected by the people:

> *The Senate of the United States shall be composed of two Senators from each State, chosen by the legislature thereof …*

In 1913 this indirect method of voting was modified by the Seventeenth Amendment, which allowed for the direct election of Senators by the "people":

> *The Senate of the United States shall be composed of two Senators from each state, elected by the people thereof.*

The first Article of the Constitution thus establishes the electoral rules, requirements, and time frames to create the representative democracy that runs the federal government and connects you, as citizen, to that government.

Article II provides for the election of the President of the United States and the formation of the Executive Branch. It established a body of participating citizens called the "electoral college," formed by legislative appointment and with a dual ballot system. Your participation indirectly selects the President. Interestingly, the initial structure allowed for the first-place finisher to become President and the second place finisher to become Vice-President. This original idea was also modified in time. The Twelfth Amendment created a single vote for President and a separate vote for Vice-President, and the political party system has made it so we have the system we are familiar with today:

> *The electors shall meet in their respective states, and vote by ballot for President and Vice-President … They shall name in their ballots the person voted for as President, and in distinct ballots the person voted for as Vice-President … The person having the greatest number of votes for President, shall be the President …*

Just as the "how" we vote has changed over time, so has "who" can vote. Reading further through the Constitution, you have the constitutional Amendments that expanded participatory democracy to the full complement of "the people." (Originally, like jury service, suffrage was limited to white male property owners of the 1780s.) Remedying the historic discrimination in voting, the Constitution expanded its participatory reach outward. The Fifteenth Amendment prohibited voting discrimination based on race.[33] The Nineteenth Amendment prohibited voting discrimination based on gender.[34] Next, the Twenty-Fourth Amendment prohibited economic barriers to voting such as the poll tax or other financial impediments. Poverty was no longer a barrier to full electoral participation.[35] Finally, the Twenty-Sixth Amendment lowered the voting age to eighteen:[36]

> *The right of citizens of the United States to vote shall not be denied or abridged by the United States or by any state*

*on account of race, color, or previous condition of servitude.
(Fifteenth Amendment)*

*The right of citizens of the United States to vote shall not be
denied or abridged by the United States or by any state on
account of sex. (Nineteenth Amendment)*

*The right of citizens of the United States to vote ... shall not
be denied or abridged by the United States or any state by
reason of failure to pay any poll tax or other tax. (Twenty-
Fourth Amendment)*

*The right of citizens of the United States, who are 18 years
of age or older, to vote, shall not be denied or abridged by the
United States or any state on account of age. (Twenty-Sixth
Amendment)*

The barriers of race, gender, poverty, and age fell over
time as social change spurred constitutional change. As
will be discussed in later chapters, this evolution had a
parallel development in who could serve on juries.

Political Participation

Constitutional participation is more than just voting (and
serving on juries). The Constitution creates and maintains space for citizens to participate in political organizations in their communities. The idea was to protect areas
of participatory activity, keeping them free from government intrusion.

Start with the First Amendment, which guarantees
individuals the right to speak about government—to participate in changing government—personally, through
petition, or through the press. You have protection for
citizens to assemble, to organize in groups, at rallies, and
through private associations:

> *Congress shall make no law abridging the freedom of speech, or of the press, or the right of the people peaceably to assemble, and to petition the government for a redress of grievances.*

The result: individuals and groups have expressed their political beliefs, shouted loudly in dissent, petitioned local, state, and federal governments, and every day since its creation protested to change the United States. As Justice Louis Brandeis recognized, the Founders hoped that actively encouraging free speech would encourage a politically engaged America:

> They believed that freedom to think as you will and to speak as you think are means indispensable to the discovery and spread of political truth; that without free speech and assembly discussion would be futile; that with them, discussion affords ordinary adequate protection against the dissemination of noxious doctrine; that the greatest menace to freedom is an inert people; that public discussion is a political duty; and that this should be a fundamental principle of the American government.[37]

Like jury service, participation to prevent an "inert" people is fundamental to our constitutional history and political freedom.

Personal Participation

Similar to the institution of jury, the Constitution encouraged participation in local organizations, including churches and civic groups.

Whatever your religious beliefs, there is little question that the Constitution envisioned strong religious *participation* in the United States. The First Amendment protects the freedom of religion by both prohibiting the establishment of a national church, and allowing freedom of conscience:

> *Congress shall make no law respecting an establishment of religion, or prohibiting the free exercise thereof . . .*

At the time of the founding, churches not only taught moral and religious values, but they were centers of education (there were few public schools) and places of community involvement.[38] Allowing people to practice their faiths meant encouraging civic participation in local settings. From the first Quaker settlements in Pennsylvania to the thousands of mega-churches across the United States today,[39] the Constitution encourages participation in community-based religious activities.

Organized religious participation mirrored other local organizations like the militia. While we now focus on the right to bear arms in the Second Amendment, the militia as a social organization required the *participation* of citizens:

> *A well regulated militia, being necessary to the security of a free state, the right of the people to keep and bear arms, shall not be infringed.*

At the time of the founding, under the Militia Act of 1792, all men between the ages of eighteen and forty-five were eligible for militia service in the states.[40] As a result, most men were required to come together and participate in the organized defense of their communities.

As you sit there as a juror, you become part of that constitutional plan of participation. The people, the vote, the church, the militia, and, of course, the jury represent the core participatory principles written into the Constitution.

Why Participation Matters
Skills of Self-Government

So, the theme of citizen participation is pretty well established in the constitutional history of the United States. The question is, why should we care about it while on jury duty?

There is a very practical answer. Participation in jury service teaches the skills required for democratic self-government.[41] Being a juror lets you develop the habits and skills of citizenship. You develop by practice. You practice by participating.

What are these "democracy" skills? Think about what is required for a politically active nation. As a juror, you are asked to "vote" based on contested facts. You must debate issues framed by contesting parties. This involves listening to others and tolerating dissenting views (as well as expressing your own opinions). Jurors necessarily expand their social interaction with different types of people, broadening perspectives, contacts, and sources of information. To apply the law, jurors must understand the law, the rights of the parties, and the legal rules guiding the decision. Each of these participatory skills—deliberation, debate, tolerance, cooperation, civility, decision making—is what we need for a democracy to work.

Each has a parallel to the political process of voting and decision making by "the people." As the Supreme Court has recognized, jury duty "affords ordinary citizens a valuable opportunity to participate in a process of government, an experience fostering, one hopes, a respect for law. Indeed, with the exception of voting, for most citizens the honor and privilege of jury duty is their most significant opportunity to participate in the democratic process."[42] For these reasons, the famed observer of

American democracy Alexis de Tocqueville stated, "The jury is both the most effective way of establishing the people's rule and the most efficient way of teaching them how to rule."[43]

As a juror, you become an official part of the justice system. Again, it is an odd concept to deputize citizens to do a job that we already employ professionals (judges) to do. But it is a purposeful decision to give power—constitutional power—to ordinary citizens. As two scholars of juries once observed:

> The Anglo-American jury is a remarkable political institution . . . It recruits a group of twelve laymen, chosen at random from the widest population; it convenes them for the purpose of the particular trial; it entrusts them with great official powers of decision; it permits them to carry on deliberations in secret and to report out their final judgment without giving reasons for it; and after their momentary service to the state has been completed, it orders them to disband and return to private life. The jury thus represents a deep commitment to the use of laymen in the administration of justice . . . it opposes the cadre of professional, experienced judges with this transient, ever-changing, ever-inexperienced group of amateurs.[44]

This sentiment recognizes that "amateurs" are the point; participation is the point. Jury service elevates regular people to the task of contributing to the government. After all, we wouldn't want professional pundits or experts as the only people who could vote in political elections. "We the People" need to be able to maintain the skills necessary to be active citizens.

One of the benefits of the courthouse in which I practiced is that judges regularly invite jurors to talk with lawyers after the case finished. The conversations range from interest in the case—why it was brought, what evidence jurors found persuasive—to more practical advice—you should shine your shoes, you did the best you could with tough facts. But often, one juror would thank the lawyers for the jury experience. It is a misplaced comment of appreciation for a juror to thank the lawyers for the experience the juror just had. But it happens, and it reflects the effects of participation—of how the juror feels rewarded, or maybe even surprised by the reward of contributing to the official act of decision. Their misdirected thanks is really an acknowledgment of the value they got out of participation.

An additional benefit of jury service is that it acts as a source of legal education for citizens. Jurors learn not only the skills of democracy, but also the substance of legal rights and the laws of the country. The judge's jury instructions may be the only time anyone formally explains the law to a nonlawyer.[45] It may be the only time anyone explains those concepts heard in movies and television of "beyond a reasonable doubt" or "burden of proof." It may be the only time that citizens have the opportunity to debate the "reasonableness" of self-defense or "negligence" in an auto accident. Tocqueville likened the jury to a free school, ever open for us to learn about governing ourselves:

> The jury contributes most powerfully to form the judgment and to increase the natural intelligence of a people, and this is, in my opinion, its greatest advantage. It may be regarded as a gratuitous public school ever open, in which every juror learns to exercise his rights . . . I do not know whether the jury is useful to those who are in litigation; but I am certain it is highly beneficial to those who decide the litigation; and I look upon it as one of the most efficacious means for the education of the people which society can employ.[46]

This institutional education was purposeful. The drafters of the Constitution had understood that juries would be the place where citizens would learn and practice the legal and political values necessary for self-government.[47] As one modern juror reflected after a criminal trial, "I truly felt that Jury Duty was the best civics lesson I've ever had. In no other way that I can think of are citizens so equally involved in the state's affairs."[48] This sentiment exemplifies the conclusion of researchers in Washington State, who conducted an exhaustive review of jury practices and attitudes to support the argument that jury service improves political participation and democratic practice.[49]

Constitutional Character

Participation as a juror says something about the person choosing to participate. It also says something about the society that lets it happen. Jury service may be a juror's only point of connection with the judicial system. The fortunate among us are not lawyers, criminal defendants, or parties to a civil lawsuit, thus most of us do not get to see how the justice system really works except as jurors. The lessons learned watching your tax dollars at work or working yourself in the jury room are things that shape society's perception of the legal system. According to studies, between 75 and 90 percent of jurors say that they had a positive experience on jury duty.[50] My informal personal polling would result in a similar high percentage. Jury service creates a "buy in" opportunity for those who have invested their time to bring home with them a positive image of the justice system (and themselves as constitutional actors). It is thus an important symbolic educational experience for the participants.

The participatory aspect of jury duty shapes our constitutional character. Those habits and skills, our civic education, helps define who we are as Americans. Being a citizen juror not only makes us better government actors in a system that expects us to participate, but it changes how we view ourselves. We see ourselves as citizens.

Again, going back to the conversation in the jury room after the verdict, there is a different sense among the jurors of having completed a job well done. No matter the verdict, it is in the air—the sense of respect for what has been accomplished. You can see the pride of having finished an unfamiliar and challenging task. You can see how the weight of judgment has changed the tone. And you can sense a special contentment that it was all done for a greater public good—that the jurors participated in their community.

In many ways, the participatory aspect of jury duty preserves the other democratic values we hold.[51] As long as someone is entrusting regular people to show up to court every day and participate in the nuts and bolts of administering justice, you can be pretty sure that they will continue to trust those same people to vote, argue about political issues, and keep on being democratically minded Americans. Just as we created the Constitution[52]—"We ordain and establish"—so we recreate the same spirit each time a jury is empanelled.[53] Each jury is a constitutional act.[54] An act of renewal. And being a juror is a reaffirmation of faith in democratic participation.

I consider trial by jury as the only anchor ever yet imagined by man, by which a government can be held to the principles of its constitution.

—Thomas Jefferson

United States Post Office (1900) Completed in 1897
SUPERVISING ARCHITECTS: Willoughby J. Edbrooke, Jeremiah O'Rourke, Charles E. Kemper, and William Martin Aiken
The United States District Court for the District of Massachusetts met here from 1926 until 1930. Razed ca. 1930.

SOURCE: NATIONAL ARCHIVES, RG 121-BA, BOX 11, PRINT 996

2

Selecting Fairness

A Faith

As you wait to see if you will be selected as a juror, look around the courtroom. Study the parties at the table. What does it say that every time two litigants appear for trial, we know one side will lose? Both sides walk into court knowing at the outset that one side will lose, yet they still show up. The stakes are even higher for criminal defendants. But day after day, both sides still appear, hopeful that they can win. The genius of our jury system was to set up a mechanism so that both sides believe that they have a fair shot at winning the case. They show up because they have faith that the system will be fair.

As a juror, your task is to make sure that such a faith is well placed. But what do we mean by fairness? For a criminal case, one answer is right there in the Sixth Amendment—"an impartial jury":

In all criminal prosecutions, the accused shall enjoy the right to a speedy and public trial, by an impartial jury of the state and district wherein the crime shall have been committed ...

Interestingly, an impartial jury is a far stretch from the earliest practice of juries. Originally, the tradition was to summon jurors who *knew* the parties to the case personally.[1] During the early reign of King Henry III, the jury consisted of witnesses who knew the litigants, the community, and the facts.[2] In the small, insulated villages of England, it made sense to allow the townsfolk who knew the parties best to decide the dispute using personal knowledge of the events. Over time, however, this practice shifted so jurors (now seen as independent judges)[3] were called to settle disputes because they had no prior knowledge of the parties.[4] By the time the jury reached America, the adversarial system had been adopted, and the goal was to find a fair and impartial jury "of one's peers" to resolve the dispute.[5]

What do we mean by impartial? If you ask the Supreme Court, "impartial" means two things in the context of jury selection. First, the jury must be selected out of "a representative cross section of the community,"[6] meaning that the jury panel must be composed of a mix of all types of people living in the community.[7] The focus is on the jury panel (or "jury venire") as a whole and not on the actual make up of any specific jury. So, you may end up with a jury of all women, but as long as the jury panel from which the all-women jury was selected had a roughly equivalent number of men and women, there is no constitutional defect. The Supreme Court has held that a defendant must show a systemic exclusion of a distinctive group from the panel to raise the claim of an unrepresentative (unconstitutional) jury.[8]

Second, the individual jurors must be unbiased, showing no personal favoritism or antipathy toward the parties.[9] In other words, a lawyer's mother, next-door neighbor, or archenemy would be "struck" as not being able to be fair to the parties. Jurors who demonstrate they cannot be fair due to a connection or predisposition to the case are struck for "just cause."

As a practicing lawyer, I had a slightly different definition of an impartial juror. It has to do with openness. I looked for "bright eyes"—a term that comes from a client who once turned to me and said, "Keep her, she's got bright eyes," meaning that the juror's wide-open earnest eyes and eagerness were so apparent that we knew she would be fair. In all other respects, she was a person I would have kept off the jury, but I deferred to my client. Empirical studies have validated my client's intuition (as did the jury verdict in that case). Scholars who study jurors have concluded that "attitudes tend to be more powerful predictors of verdict choices than demographic characteristics."[10]

Voir Dire

So, what happens as you wait to be selected for a jury? You go through a process of jury selection called "voir dire." The term refers to the oath to tell the truth,[11] but in practice it is a way to find those individuals who can be fair and impartial in this particular case. The series of questions you are asked are all focused on one purpose: to see if you can be fair.

In some court systems, these questions are asked in lengthy questionnaires prior to arriving in court; other courts use a system of group questioning in the courtroom or individual questioning in the judge's chambers. Sometimes the judge does the questioning, sometimes the judge and lawyers, and in certain jurisdictions the lawyers get to do all the questioning. In most federal courts, the judge controls the questions. In some free-wheeling state courts, a lawyer friend likened it to a day-time talk show in her question-and-answer sessions with potential jurors.

Like daytime television, sometimes the questions asked can be embarrassing or revealing. To have a judge ask about a personal trauma in a room full of strangers creates real hardship. But there is a good reason behind the questions. The parties need to know the truth about you, even the unpleasant truth. That is why you swear the oath. That is why, hopefully, the judge is sensitive to the balance between candor and privacy concerns.[12] It is not so much about you, but about the fairness to the parties that necessitates this real loss of privacy.

In many jurisdictions, the only information the lawyers have about you before voir dire is your name, age, and occupation. This is why millions of dollars are spent on "jury consultants,"[13] who study your demographic makeup, educational level, and probably the bags under your eyes to determine a stereotypical and likely superficial composite of whether you will be fair (or better yet, sympathetic to their side). The process of jury selection requires lawyers to intuit who you are from evaluating the superficial you.[14]

Beyond demographic information, scour the minds of trial lawyers and you would likely uncover a taxonomy of haircuts, a superstition about women's shoes, and an unscientific compendium on various perfumes and what they say about a particular person. This lesson becomes fixed in the eyes of lawyers who peg you based on your suit, newspaper, or personal style. My father likes to tell the story of my first jury summons when I went unknowingly with a copy of Scott Turow's latest novel. I wasn't picked for the criminal jury. The book I carried up to meet the lawyers was *Presumed Innocent*.

No matter the system chosen for voir dire, you are asked if you know the parties in the case, the lawyers, or the judge. You are asked if you have heard about the case, read newspaper articles about it, or know any of the witnesses. In some cases, issues of pretrial publicity can overwhelm the proceedings. More than six hundred jurors were queried for potential service in what was to be a well-known sports figure's rape trial because of the nonstop press surrounding the case.[15] The case was dismissed before trial, but that was not even the biggest jury panel ever. That award goes to a capital murder case in California where 864 prospective jurors were queried in the search for a jury that had not prejudged the case.[16]

In criminal voir dire, you are asked if the subject matter—murder, assault, financial fraud—is such that you cannot be fair. Of course, everyone has feelings that murder, assault, and financial fraud are bad, but the question is whether the nature of the crime so affects you that it closes off your ability to be reasoned and impartial. In civil voir dire, you might be asked if you have connection or special knowledge about the industry, accident, or type of lawsuit at issue. Finally, you are asked if you have any religious or moral beliefs that will keep you from serving. Depending on the jurisdiction, this process of being questioned can last hours or days.[17]

Do not feel insulted if you are not chosen to sit on the jury. I have rejected people because they wore sweater vests or loud ties, and I have kept people because of the neighborhood in which they grew up or went to school. It is not a personal rejection (except for the ties); it is a function of trying to find people who feel right to the parties. Remember, as a juror you know very little about the expected evidence or witnesses, and it might be a tactical decision having nothing to do with you as a person that keeps you off the jury.

One of my favorite parts of jury selection is seeing what excuses people come up with to be excused from jury service. It is telling both about people's views of their civic responsibility and their ideas of fairness. Some are simply obvious, claiming they have already prejudged the case, the defendant, or the particular business being sued. Some are humorous, saying "my cat needs me,"[18] "I dislike lawyers,"[19] or "Judge, I think this will conflict with my trial before *you* next Thursday." Some are both—a juror's prayer was once recorded:

A Juror's Prayer

Dear God, please give me an excuse in a hurry,
Something good to keep me off this stupid jury.
My job! My kids! My sick Aunt Bea!
Who could survive even a day without me?
And you should know, by the way, I'm deaf in one ear,
So when a witness testifies, I won't be able to hear.
Here comes the defense lawyer, eyes right on me.
"Just because my client's been charged, do you think he's guilty?"
"Actually, I do," I say, trying hard not to smirk.
"If not of this crime, then because he's a jerk!"
But be warned, Mr. State Attorney, don't think I'll help you,
You see, I hate the police, informants, and prosecutors, too!
Now is the time, the voir dire est fini,
Please, God, don't let them pick me.
Did I mention I'm scheduled for brain surgery?[20]

The excuses are a daily occurrence, making it harder for the lawyers to choose a jury consistent with the constitutional principle of impartiality.[21]

Trial Fairness

Jury selection is only the beginning. All through the trial proceedings, there are systemic attempts to ensure fairness. If you are selected for the jury, the judge will read to you the rules of law that govern trials. In a criminal case, you will be instructed to apply the presumption of innocence—a presumption dating back to the time of Moses, as recorded in the Book of Deuteronomy.[22] The presumption means that even though you are sitting through a pretty long trial brought by government lawyers who seem pretty sure of themselves, and even though the evidence seems pretty overwhelming, you still—as a matter of law—are required to view the defendant as innocent. It is a strange and counterintuitive instruction that underscores the importance of juror impartiality.

In addition, you will be instructed on how to view an expert's testimony, or a perjurer's testimony, or conflicting testimony. And you will be told that during the entire trial proceedings you may not conduct independent research, check out the crime scene, talk to witnesses, or even speak to other jurors about the case except when all of you are present for final deliberations. Only then, only all together, can you discuss the case.[23] Finally, you will be given the jury instructions from which you must apply the facts to the law and reach a verdict based on the evidence. These are the rules. Rules of fairness.

Fairness and the Constitution
Constitutional Fairness

Legal instructions provide rules of fairness for jurors, yet there are other fairness rules—constitutional rules— that frame the work the lawyers do in trial. First, the fact that there are lawyers in court reflects a constitutional recognition of fairness. The Sixth Amendment guarantees a right to a lawyer in a criminal case:

> *In all criminal prosecutions, the accused shall enjoy the right . . . to have the assistance of counsel for his defense.*

The rationale is that if the state has paid lawyers representing its interests, then as a matter of fairness the accused should also have access to legal assistance.

Similarly, you may not realize why you have to listen to the repetitive testimony of each police officer who was involved in the case, or why the defense lawyer appears to be asking so many questions, but the right to confront witnesses through "the crucible of cross-examination"[24] is at the core of the Sixth Amendment's Confrontation Clause.

> *The accused shall enjoy the right ... to be confronted with the witnesses against him.*

Gone are the days when an enemy of the state could be convicted solely on the basis of sworn statements submitted to the court, rather than live testimony. The right to confront witnesses in court was established in reaction to infamous cases such as the 1603 treason trial of Sir Walter Raleigh, in which Raleigh had been convicted on the basis of the written statements of Lord Cobham.[25] At trial, Raleigh accused Cobham of lying to save himself. Demanding that Cobham be brought to the trial, Raleigh challenged the fairness of the proceeding: "The Proof of the Common Law is by witness and jury: let Cobham be here, let him speak it. Call my accuser before my face ..."[26] However, it was not to be; Cobham's letter of accusation was all the evidence the jury used to convict and condemn Raleigh. The lesson of the Sir Walter Raleigh case echoed in the Founding era and is still discussed and cited by the Supreme Court today.[27] Now, the Lord Cobhams of the world are required to come into court and look into the eyes of the defendant and the jury and make their accusation. This requirement of confrontation is based on the rationale that juries can best judge the credibility of witnesses by seeing them answer tough questions at trial.

The right to confrontation is coupled with the Sixth Amendment right to "compulsory process," meaning that the Constitution guarantees the accused the right to call witnesses (and compel them to show up) for his or her defense:

> In all criminal prosecutions, the accused shall enjoy the right … to have compulsory process for obtaining witnesses in his favor.

In an adversarial system, both sides need to be able to call witnesses in support of their arguments to make the system fairly balanced.

In a criminal case, these Sixth Amendment rights are combined with established rules of fair process referred to as "due process requirements." The constitutional guarantee to a jury trial in federal and state court is one such due process right.[28] These trial rules located in both the Fifth and Fourteenth Amendments govern matters such as of burdens of proof (who needs to convince you), the standard of proof (to what standard you need to be convinced), the presumption of innocence, and the fact that the accused need not testify for his or her own defense, and that this silence cannot be held against the defense:

> No person shall be … deprived of life, liberty, or property, without due process of law. (Fifth Amendment)

> Nor shall any State deprive any person of life, liberty, or property without due process of law. (Fourteenth Amendment)

> No person … shall be compelled in any criminal case to be a witness against himself. (Fifth Amendment)

The Founders understood that a fair criminal system equalizes the unequal power of the state prosecuting an individual for a crime.

Rule of Law

Trial rights are but a portion of the constitutional commitment to fairness. Pick up a copy of the United States Constitution and you have tangible proof of fairness. The task of writing down our fundamental laws wasn't just to preserve the ideas of the past, but to inform us of the ground rules for our future government.

The limitations on government were memorialized in a written document. The "rule of law" is literally written down. It doesn't have to be this way. The British Constitution exists as an uncodified collection of rules that includes the Magna Carta, the English Bill of Rights of 1687, Acts of Parliament, and the common law.[29] But our Constitution is written down, providing clear notice of the rules of constitutional order. The Founders emphasized the importance of process—the formal rules that organize, protect, and constrain the government.

Fairness Rules

In some ways it should not be a surprise that our Constitution emphasizes fairness. The American Revolution was in part a revolution against the unfairness of British taxes, policing, and royal policy. Perhaps the greatest theme that runs throughout the United States Constitution is the protection against arbitrary police power. The protections run from how criminal charges can be brought, through trial, and to after criminal sentencing. Rights of fair notice, fair process, and fair punishment are constitutionally established:

> *The accused shall enjoy the right ... to be informed of the nature and cause of the accusation. (Sixth Amendment)*

No person shall be held to answer for a capital, or other infamous crime, unless on a presentment or indictment of a grand jury. (Fifth Amendment)

Excessive bail shall not be required, nor excessive fines imposed, nor cruel and unusual punishment inflicted. (Eighth Amendment)

The Constitution sets the bar for fair treatment of all citizens, even the least powerful. And when the government does take our most precious right—our freedom—we have the right to petition the courts to hear our requests for release and our complaints of unfairness through the habeas corpus procedure:

The privilege of the writ of habeas corpus shall not be suspended, unless when in cases of rebellion or invasion the public safety may require it. (Article I, Section 9)

This ancient privilege allows people in custody to request that the government justify the deprivation of their liberty. From the Latin, it means "you have the body," and it acts "as a fundamental instrument for safeguarding individual freedom against arbitrary and lawless state action."[30] Today, it protects individuals who have been held without charge, those held pretrial because of excessive bail, and those seeking to challenge their state convictions in federal court.

Similarly, Article I, Section 9, of the Constitution prevents Congress from even passing certain types of unfair laws:

No bill of attainder or ex post facto law shall be passed.

Bills of attainder were laws that singled out individuals for criminal punishment or death. The English

Parliament (and a few American colonial legislatures) had given themselves the power to punish as they deemed fit—almost always targeting those who disagreed with the lawmakers.[31] As late as the American Revolution, hundreds of Tory sympathizers had their land confiscated by acts of attainder.[32] Similarly, ex post facto laws were retroactive actions designed to make something that had not been previously criminal subject to criminal penalties. This type of law usually had been passed to punish enemies of the current government.[33] In restricting this type of punishment power, the Founders signaled their condemnation of unfair laws.

Civil Fairness

In the same way the Constitution precludes Congress from singling out people for punishment, it also precludes Congress from unfairly taking property away from citizens. At a minimum, the state must pay us just compensation for any loss of private property:

> *Nor shall private property be taken for public use, without just compensation. (Fifth Amendment)*

Further, property interests are explicitly protected by the Seventh Amendment's guarantee of a civil jury. The Founding generation cared deeply about the civil jury. One of the concerns after passing the original Constitution was the lack of any constitutional provision for civil juries. Anti-Federalists took this omission as an ominous sign that the new federal government had designs to abolish the civil jury.[34] To quell the concern, jury trials in civil cases were specifically protected in the Seventh Amendment:

> *In suits at common law ... the right of trial by jury shall be preserved.*

Historically, it had been the civil jury as much as the criminal jury that had stood as an institution of liberty.[35] The same protections of notice, a hearing, rules of procedure, and an impartial final decision maker were central to the protection against potential unfairness. On jury duty in any civil trial, you become part of that historic thread—impartial, representative, fair, and constitutionally required.

Why Fair Process Matters
The Individual Case

In the trenches of criminal court, it is pretty easy to see why fairness matters. On one side, you have a real person who has one chance, one trial, one trip through the legal system. Before every jury trial, there is a moment of expectation as I stand looking through the bars of the holding cell behind the courtroom. I look into my client's eyes and see the hope for a fair process, a fair judge, a fair result. On the other side, you have the witnesses, the victim, the victim's family, who also have only one chance for accountability and closure. On both sides, you can feel the nervous emotion heightened by the wait for the start of the trial.

Similarly, in civil cases, fairness matters. The civil litigants usually have spent years (sometimes decades) waiting for a resolution to their dispute—compensation for an injury, back pay for discrimination, settlement of a contract. Both sides expect a legitimate outcome. Both sides are waiting for a jury to assess their claims fairly.

One of the difficulties in practicing in a particular area of the law is that the professionals sometimes forget that even though they might have hundreds of cases, it is the client's only case. Professionals get used to the routine, to the rhythms of court, forgetting how novel the experience is for each client. This is another benefit of juries. Juries— by design and practice—look at the case fresh. Just like the litigants, it is the juror's only case. Judge Shirley Abrahamson, Chief Justice of the Wisconsin Supreme Court, once was selected for a jury while a sitting judge. In an essay on her experience (which was quite positive), she explained that it is this openness and freshness of the jury that allows for fair outcomes.[36] She ended her essay quoting an observation about courts of law from a century earlier:

> And the horrible thing about all legal officials, even the best, about all judges, magistrates, barristers, detectives, and policemen, is not that they are wicked (some of them are good), not that they are stupid (several of them are quite intelligent), it is simply that they have got used to it. . . . They do not see the awful court of judgment; they only see their own workshop.[37]

Jury service reboots the system and allows the litigants to have their positions fairly evaluated by those who have not gotten used to it. For jurors, each case is new. Each case is treated anew.

The Societal Benefit

Fairness goes beyond simply judging a case impartially; it has a much greater benefit to society—acceptance of the rule of law. If you think about it, societies have used all sorts of dispute resolution mechanisms in the past. In early days we had trials by combat, ranging from duels to wars. We experimented with the "trial by ordeal."[38] One such ordeal was "trial by water," in which the "accused" had a rock tied to his leg and was thrown into a lake— if he was "guilty" he would float and be convicted, if he was "innocent" he would sink.[39] (Think about that for a second.) The choice of having twelve randomly selected people decide your fate in accordance with written, public laws is vastly preferable to these kinds of alternatives.

The jury system as we know it is the result of a long struggle and relatively recent success. Even our process of formalized written jury instructions did not begin until the 1920s and 1930s.[40]

So why do we have a jury system based on the rule of law? There are three main benefits: it is (1) workable, (2) fixable, and (3) legitimate.

Any system of justice has to work. That means the legal system has to be efficient enough to respond to meet the challenge of resolving disputes. The words "efficiency" and jury duty do not always go hand in hand. Yet tens of thousands of trials are processed through juries each year.[41] The criminal justice system affects millions of people nationwide.[42]

But "workable" doesn't just mean efficient. Making a dispute resolution system workable in a democracy means making sure citizens can see how it works. A fair process involves notice, transparency, consistency, and established rules. What that means is that the application and enforcement of established laws is open for all to see, and the rules are applied evenly no matter who happens to run afoul of the law. As Chief Justice John Marshall wrote, echoing John Adams's draft of the Massachusetts Constitution of 1778, "The government of the United States has been emphatically termed a government of laws, and not of men."[43] Contracts get enforced, commercial systems can predict likely outcomes, and society feels safer because lawbreakers go to jail. We also have a much better way of resolving conflict than duels at sundown or superstitious rituals. While inequity and corruption exist, we have enforceable rules to eradicate them. Compared to many countries without the rule of law, we live with a greater sense of certainty about the rules governing society.

"Certainty" does not mean it is perfect. We know it is not. But it is fixable. Precisely because our law is written down and made public, we can change it when it doesn't work. Like the Constitution, one of the differences in our system is that we can challenge the law when it fails to live up to its promise. Thomas Jefferson once wrote, "Written constitutions may be violated in moments of passion or delusion, yet they furnish a text to which those who are watchful may again rally and recall the people."[44] In a democracy, if you believe a law to be unfair you can work to change it.

This ability to change an unfair law is part of what gives the legal system legitimacy. So does a jury. A jury allows citizens, themselves, to be the arbiters of fairness in the legal system. Justice Hugo Black explained, "The institution of the jury . . . places the real direction of society in the hands of the governed . . . The jury injects a democratic element into the law. This element is vital to the effective administration of criminal justice, not only in safeguarding the rights of the accused, but in encouraging popular acceptance of the laws and the necessary general acquiescence in their application."[45] We accept that our law is fair because we had a hand in applying it.

A juror once confided that she was a cynic by nature and had approached jury duty accordingly. However, once she got in the jury room things changed. She explained that before that moment, she didn't think her ideas would be taken seriously. She didn't really think the system would be fair. Before that moment, she hadn't really thought about what a trial would be like or why it would matter. But suddenly she was forced to decide. Right there, right now. She had to think. She had to care. She had to be the one to make it fair. And most important, she saw that other people cared about what she had to say, and because of that trust she was able to shape a just outcome. Still a cynic, she laughed that she trusted the system so long as she was a part of it.

Adversarial Justice

If you are ever bored sitting in federal criminal court, look around and count the people who are present because of the United States Constitution. The defense lawyer is there because the Sixth Amendment guarantees the "accused" counsel. The prosecutors representing the United States of America have authority through Article II, which grants prosecuting authority to the Executive Branch. The judge is empowered through Article III to interpret the law. Your fellow jurors exist because of the Sixth Amendment and Article III's explicit protection of a criminal jury. Even the spectators sitting in the "public trial" are allowed to watch because of the Constitution. With the exception of the court reporter and the clerk, all the jobs have been constitutionally ordained.

These roles—including yours—exist to further the ideal of fairness and due process. A defense lawyer is ethically bound to "zealously advocate" for a client.[46] A prosecutor is ethically bound "to do justice."[47] A judge promises to uphold the Constitution impartially.[48] Each juror raises his or her hand and swears an oath to apply the law faithfully. In fact, "the term juror comes from the Latin root *juro*, which means I swear."[49]

The hope is that this process—with its conflicting adversarial interests and roles—will create a just outcome. The theory is that if each person in that room does his or her job, the legal system becomes stronger. It is a constitutional hope, as the Preamble to the Constitution seeks to "establish justice":

> We the People of the United States, in order to form a more perfect union, establish Justice, . . . , do ordain and establish this Constitution for the United States of America.

Of course, all the Constitution established was a system, not an outcome.

One of the more unlikely yet revealing stories in the history of constitutional law is the case involving Clarence Earl Gideon—a man who demanded fairness. American history is filled with important letters and correspondence. Rarely, however, does a jailhouse letter drafted by an uneducated drifter change the country. Yet a single letter written by Clarence Earl Gideon changed the Sixth Amendment and our expectation of fairness.[50] Accused of stealing five dollars and a few bottles of beer from a Panama City pool hall, Gideon, a petty thief and high school dropout, was sentenced to five years in a Florida jail.[51] The only problem was that Gideon happened to be innocent. In 1961, if you were accused of a crime and were too poor to hire a lawyer, you were required to represent yourself in court. That meant that people like Gideon had to try to convince a judge (or jury) of their innocence without any legal help. Gideon wasn't a very good advocate and he quickly found himself in jail. So he did something quite unusual. He wrote a letter directly to the Supreme Court of the United States complaining of the unfairness of his conviction. In that handwritten document he complained that he didn't have a lawyer and that it was wrong to incarcerate him without a fair trial. Perhaps more amazingly, the Supreme Court read the letter and agreed to decide whether people like Gideon had a constitutional right to a lawyer free of charge. The Supreme Court appointed lawyers, heard arguments, and eventually reversed Gideon's conviction with a legal decision that held that all people accused of felony crimes were entitled to be represented by a lawyer. It's still the law of the land.

Gideon's story has a happy ending because the Supreme Court not only overturned his conviction, but Gideon was acquitted at the retrial (the prosecutor's main witness turned out to be the likely thief). Of course, it did not have to turn out that way. The Supreme Court could have agreed that Gideon deserved a lawyer, but Gideon might have been found guilty anyway. The case stands as a landmark decision because of its creation of a process, not because of the result.

To get both a fair process and a fair result, each of the people in that courtroom must practice the principle of fairness. A system of due process works only if we do. Process alone is not enough. Throughout American history, the legal process upheld slavery, segregation laws, and the internment of Japanese citizens in World War II.[52] In 2000, the legal system allowed shameful prosecutions like those in Tulia, Texas, in which 20 percent of the African American population (thirty-eight people) was arrested and charged with selling cocaine, based on the inconsistent and uncorroborated word of one discredited police officer.[53] The legal system in the twenty-first century tried and convicted them—due process and all—and many were sentenced to decades in jail before the fraud and lies were exposed. Process did not mean justice to them.[54]

In many ways, the operational (if not intended) key word in the Preamble may be "establish," and not "justice"—that the Constitution's goal was to establish the process for justice, not simply decree it into being. The rest is left to citizens and jurors, who must practice and live the constitutional ideal of fairness every day in court.

Equal opportunity to participate in the fair administration of justice is fundamental to our democratic system. It not only furthers the goals of the jury system. It reaffirms the promise of equality under the law—that all citizens, regardless of race, ethnicity, or gender, have the chance to take part directly in our democracy. . . . When persons are excluded from participation in our democratic process solely because of race or gender, this promise of equality dims, and the integrity of our judicial system is jeopardized.
—*J. E. B. v. Alabama*, 511 U.S. 127, 145–46 (1994)

Public Building (n.d., ca. 1905) Completed in 1905
SUPERVISING ARCHITECT: James Knox Taylor
The United States District Court for the District of Wyoming met here until 1933; the United States Circuit Court for the District of Wyoming met here until that court was abolished in 1912; the United States Court of Appeals for the Eighth Circuit met here until 1933. Razed ca. 1966.

SOURCE: NATIONAL ARCHIVES, RG 121-BS, BOX 97, FOLDER QQ, PRINT 42

3

Choosing Equality

A Number

Throughout your jury service, you are known by a number—a juror number. You respond to that number. There are no nicknames or familiarities on jury duty. In the same way there are no titles. Whether you are a soccer mom or a Senator (or both), you are simply a number to the jury system. The number is not meant to insult, but to equalize. It provides the anonymity of being a citizen, one of millions who are doing exactly what you are doing in court: waiting for his or her number to be called. In 2003, during a federal gang shooting case, there was a bit of excitement over juror number 142. In the juror questionnaire, under former occupation, the juror had listed "President of the United States." The juror had also stated that he could be impartial notwithstanding his "unusual experience with the O.I.C." (Office of the Independent Counsel).[1] Yet, had former President William Jefferson

Clinton been asked to serve, he would have entered that service as number 142, equal to the other eleven members of that jury.

Equality is central to our democracy and to our jury system, and the battles to ensure a nondiscriminatory system have been fought throughout our history. Jury duty, like voting rights, began as the provenance of white, property-owning men, and only slowly evolved into a more inclusive, diverse institution. Today, legal equality remains a central victory in the struggle for civil rights. It is a relatively recent victory, and one that connects back to the ideals of our founding documents. To understand how seriously the legal system takes the principle of a nondiscriminatory practice in today's jury selection, you must see it in the context of the plainly racist, sexist, and class-based history leading up to this egalitarian view. But, most important, you must see it as your right as a juror.

Yes, equality during jury selection is *your* constitutional right.[2] Even though you might naturally assume the voir dire process is conducted only to protect the defendants' or litigants' rights at trial, it also protects the right of jurors not to be excluded. While you cannot sue to enforce this right, and you must rely on the parties to challenge it, its existence recognizes the important role you play in the jury.[3] So, as you sit there hoping that you constitute an excludable class with too much going on in your life to be on jury duty, remember that the fuss and bother is partially about you.

A Juror's Right

To understand this focus on a juror's constitutional right, consider two Supreme Court cases involving racial equality and juries.

Case 1: In Jefferson City, Kentucky, an African American man, James Batson, was charged with second-degree burglary and receipt of stolen goods.[4] During the voir dire process, the prosecuting attorney struck the only four African American jurors on the panel. Batson's lawyer objected because the strikes appeared to be based on race, and it left Batson facing an all-white jury. The trial court denied the objection and Batson went to trial and lost. He challenged the prosecutor's use of racially based preemptory challenges all the way to the Supreme Court.[5]

In *Batson v. Kentucky*, the Supreme Court decided that the state's purposeful racial discrimination violated the Equal Protection Clause of the Fourteenth Amendment. The Court held that the state could not exclude jurors on account of race. The Court explained that purposeful racial discrimination "violates a defendant's right to equal protection because it denies him the protection that a trial by jury is intended to secure. 'The very idea of a jury is a body . . . composed of the peers or equals of the person whose rights it is selected or summoned to determine; that is, of his neighbors, fellows, associates, persons having the same legal status in society as that which he holds.'"[6] In other words, to get a fair trial, you needed a jury of your peers, including people of all races.

But then the Court went further, connecting the harm of discrimination to the rights of the prospective juror:

Racial discrimination in selection of jurors harms not only the accused whose life or liberty they are summoned to try. . . . [B]y denying a person participation in jury service on account of his race, the State unconstitutionally discriminated *against the excluded juror*. . . . The harm from discriminatory jury selection extends beyond that inflicted on the defendant and the excluded juror to touch the entire community. Selection procedures that purposefully exclude black persons from juries undermine public confidence in the fairness of our system of justice.[7]

The Court ruled that discriminatory jury selection violated the Fourteenth Amendment's guarantee of equal protection of the laws, thus directly addressing the exclusion of African Americans from participation in civil society. Based on its holding, the Supreme Court reversed Mr. Batson's criminal conviction.[8]

Case 2: In Franklin County, Ohio, Larry Joe Powers, a white man, faced trial on two counts of aggravated murder and one count of attempted aggravated murder with a firearm.[9] During the jury selection process, the state prosecutor struck six African American jurors. Powers's lawyer objected to the racially based strikes, notwithstanding that Powers was white and the case did not involve any racial issues. The judge denied the objection. Mr. Powers challenged the prosecutor's strikes as being a violation of the same principle that granted James Batson a new trial. The question for the Supreme Court was whether it mattered that Powers was white and was challenging the striking of people of a different race.

In *Powers v. Ohio*, the Court reversed Mr. Powers' convictions based on the injury done to the *jurors'* constitutional rights:

> We hold that the Equal Protection Clause prohibits a prosecutor from using the State's peremptory challenges to exclude otherwise qualified and unbiased persons from the petit jury solely by reason of their race, a practice that forecloses a significant opportunity to participate in civic life. An individual juror does not have a right to sit on any particular petit jury, but he or she does possess the right not to be excluded from one on account of race.[10]

The race of the defendant did not matter. What mattered was the injury done to the jury system and the jurors themselves. A murder conviction was reversed because of the constitutional rights of the excluded jurors.[11]

To get a sense of just how far the Supreme Court has gone in upholding this nondiscriminatory policy based on constitutional equality, the Court has also prevented *a defendant* from using race-based preemptory challenges.[12] Both *Batson* and *Powers* involved the state prosecutor making race-based strikes of jurors (presumably to benefit a state prosecution). But in *Georgia v. McCollum*, the Supreme Court held that a defendant—the individual facing the power of the state—cannot purposefully use race to choose jurors, even in a case in which race is a factor.[13]

This rule of nondiscrimination applies not only to criminal cases, but also to civil cases between two private litigants.[14] In addition, the Supreme Court has applied this rule to other types of discrimination as well.[15] Just as lawyers cannot strike jurors based on race, lawyers cannot strike jurors based on gender. In *J. E. B. v. Alabama*, the Supreme Court held that "gender . . . is an unconstitutional proxy for juror competence and impartiality."[16] The Court again reaffirmed the harm done to the litigants, the community, and the individual jurors in the jury panel:

> All persons, when granted the opportunity to serve on a jury, have the right not to be excluded summarily because of discriminatory and stereotypical presumptions that reflect and reinforce patterns of historical discrimination. Striking individual jurors on the assumption that they hold particular views simply because of their gender is "practically a brand upon them, affixed by the law, an assertion of their inferiority." It denigrates the dignity of the excluded juror, and, for a woman, re-invokes a history of exclusion from political participation. The message it sends to all those in the courtroom, and all those who may later

learn of the discriminatory act, is that certain individuals, for no reason other than gender, are presumed unqualified by state actors to decide important questions upon which reasonable persons could disagree.[17]

The protection again runs to the individual juror and not simply the parties in court. It is a juror's constitutional right and protection. It is your right.

The cases above were all decided in the last part of the twentieth century and, in part, were the product of the political, social, and cultural change in racial and gender roles. Yet each case reflects the constitutional value of equality—a contested term in actual practice, but one that is part of our constitutional structure.

Equality and the Constitution
History of Inequality

Why has the Supreme Court gone so far to protect equality in jury service? In part, it is because the history of the jury has been anything but equal.

Two years after the Constitution was signed in 1787, and before the Bill of Rights was enacted in 1791, the new federal government passed the Federal Judiciary Act of 1789.[18] In addition to setting up the federal court system and creating the position of Attorney General,[19] this Act allowed the states to decide juror qualifications. The result, not surprisingly, was that each state adopted different juror requirements to serve.[20] One inequity these laws shared, however, was the exclusion of African Americans and women from jury service.

Before the Civil War, African Americans were excluded from juries in every state except Massachusetts.[21] More than seventy years passed from the signing of the Constitution before the first recorded African American was seated in a Massachusetts courthouse.[22] Following the Civil War, the nation enacted three constitutional amendments to remove the "badges of slavery"[23] from civil society. Yet the Reconstruction Amendments (the Thirteenth, Fourteenth, and Fifteenth) did not change the actual practice of racial discrimination in jury selection. Although Congress passed the Civil Rights Act of 1875, which made it a criminal offense to exclude jurors based on race,[24] it had little real-world effect. Similarly ignored was the Supreme Court's *Strauder v. West Virginia* decision, which held that racial discrimination in jury selection violated the Fourteenth Amendment.[25] It was not until the civil rights movement of the 1960s and the social changes in the twentieth century that discrimination eased in courtrooms and jury panels across the United States.[26]

The core problem lay in a selection processes that had been designed to keep African Americans off the lists of prospective jurors. States did not need an explicit law barring African Americans from sitting on a jury if they simply kept certain names off the jury list. If you weren't on the list, you couldn't be selected as a juror. Post-Reconstruction tolerance of local discriminatory practices became commonplace. Jeffrey Abramson, in his book *We the Jury: The Jury System and the Ideal of Democracy*, lists some of the starkest inequities.[27] In one Kentucky county in 1938, no African American had been summoned for jury duty (grand or petit) for thirty-two years, even though one-sixth of the population was African American. In one Louisiana county in 1947, no African American had served in twenty years. In Mississippi, a county had qualified only 25 out of 12,511 African Americans for jury service, and no African American had served in the last thirty years.[28]

The reason, again, was the juror selection system. Traditionally called a "key-man"[29] or "blue-ribbon"[30] system, these selection methods allowed local officials to handpick "qualified" jurors for their jury lists. While

most overtly biased in southern states, these discretion-
ary juror requirements were found throughout the country.[31] In 1903 in Maine, municipal officers qualified only
jurors who were considered people of "good moral character, of approved integrity, of sound judgment and well
informed."[32] In Pennsylvania, jurors were chosen if they
were suitably "sober, intelligent, and judicious persons,"
and jury commissioners were required to eliminate those
deemed "decrepit, ignorant, [or] intemperate."[33] Such sub-
jective requirements gave officials leeway to choose from
only a limited subset of the population. Even though the
Supreme Court overturned a criminal conviction almost
every year from 1935 to 1975 based on a claim of unconstitutional jury discrimination,[34] this type of systemic racial
discrimination in jury selection mocked the premise of
equality under law.[35]

The same pattern of discrimination existed against
women. Women were disqualified from being jurors by
law in almost every state in the nation until the twentieth century. Indeed, the 1880 Supreme Court decision
in *Strauder v. West Virginia*, which was the first victory
against racial discrimination in jury selection, explicitly
authorized discrimination against women, providing
that states could confine jury panels "to males."[36] While
certain states allowed women to serve on juries before
the passage of the Nineteenth Amendment—specifically
Utah (1898), Washington (1911), Kansas (1912), Nevada
(1914), California (1917), and Michigan (1918)—most
states did not, and the federal system did not protect a
woman's right to serve until 1957.[37]

Even after the Nineteenth Amendment was ratified in
1920, states continued to discourage or prevent women
from serving as jurors. Usually, this was through the
establishment of "volunteer" selection systems, meaning
a mandatory jury service for men and a voluntary jury
service for women.[38] In 1947 the Supreme Court upheld

a New York law that allowed a special exemption for women if they simply chose not to serve as jurors.[39] Similarly, in 1961 the Court upheld a Florida law that automatically exempted women (not men) from jury duty and required women (not men) affirmatively to register to be a part of the jury pool.[40] Depending on the state, women were precluded from serving on juries for a host of sexist reasons. Such excuses included that the subject matter of trials would pollute the minds of "proper" women,[41] that women would neglect their home and children,[42] or that women were not as qualified as men.[43] As late as 1957, Alabama, Mississippi, South Carolina, and West Virginia simply barred women from serving on juries altogether.[44]

All this changed in 1975, with the Supreme Court's decision in *Taylor v. Louisiana*, which held that the Constitution is violated when women are systemically excluded from jury service.[45] Billy J. Taylor was a man challenging the absence of women on his jury. Mr. Taylor showed that of the 1,800 jurors summoned to jury service in the year before his trial, a grand total of twelve were women. And of the 175 jurors selected for his jury panel, none were women.[46] The Supreme Court agreed with Mr. Taylor, and in a decision that judicially ended jury inequality for women, it reversed the conviction and sent a clear message about equality: "If the fair cross-section rule is to govern the selection of juries, as we have concluded it must, women cannot be systematically excluded from jury panels from which petit juries are drawn."[47]

Congress had attempted to address this systemic pattern of gender inequality through the Civil Rights Act of 1957, which provided that women could serve on federal juries and that jury service was no longer dependent on state laws.[48] And, for all practical purposes, Congress ended the pattern of racial inequality by enacting the Jury Selection and Service Act of 1968, which required federal courts to adopt a random selection process for jurors.[49]

A computer or equivalent random selection method now chooses potential jurors. Following the federal lead, most state jurisdictions use some combination of voter registration rolls, actual voter lists, property tax lists, unemployment compensation recipient lists, driver's license databases, and a mixture of other municipal data sources to come up with juror lists.[50] By taking the matter out of the hands of community "key-men" and by eliminating undefined qualifications for "qualified" jurors, juror selection systems have became more objective and equal. As Congress stated in its passage of the 1968 Act:

> It must be remembered that the jury is designed not only to understand the case, but also to reflect the community's sense of justice in deciding it. As long as there are significant departures from the cross-sectional goal, biased juries are the result—biased in the sense that they reflect a slanted view of the community they are supposed to represent.[51]

The history of jury inequality helps explain the Supreme Court's hard-line stance on ending discrimination in jury selection.

Given this unequal history, why do we consider the principle of equality to be a constitutional ideal? It is a question worth reflecting on during your jury service, because you now represent the result of this long struggle toward equality.

An Aspiration

The original Constitution is an imperfect model of equality. While the Founders concerned themselves with an egalitarian and progressive republican government for free white males, the document also included an immoral compromise on slavery. Right there in the text of Article

I, Section 2, existed the calculus that devalued hundreds of thousands of Americans:

> *Representatives and direct taxes shall be apportioned among the several states which may be included within this union, according to their respective numbers, which shall be determined by adding to the whole number of free persons, including those bound to service for a term of years, and excluding Indians not taxed, three fifths of all other persons.*

The "three fifths" compromise—treating slaves as less than a full free person—remained a stain on the Founding ideals until the Civil War and the Reconstruction Amendments.

The chasm between the ideals of equality and the practice of slaveholding is a subject that numerous scholars have addressed in detail,[52] and is beyond the scope of this chapter. For our purposes, the question is, how can one say that the Constitution stands for the principle of equality in the face of the historical facts?

Two answers respond to this legitimate criticism. The first, less satisfying answer, is that the ideal of equality for white men created the foundation for the equality of all "the People." In his famous "I Have a Dream" speech, Martin Luther King Jr. articulated this optimistic view of the Founders' intent:

> When the architects of our republic wrote the magnificent words of the Constitution and the Declaration of Independence, they were signing a promissory note to which every American was to fall heir. This note was a promise that all men—yes, black men as well as white men—would be guaranteed the unalienable rights of life, liberty, and the pursuit of happiness.[53]

By incorporating the Declaration of Independence's self-evident truth "that all men are created equal" into our constitutional ideals, King was able to elide the Constitution's textual reality of inequality. He also could recreate a new understanding using the language and ideals of the original Founding. As Azar Nafisi has written, picking up on the theme and work of Martin Luther King Jr.:

It has been pointed out that the man who wrote the Declaration of Independence—who could state with simplicity and beauty that every individual has the right to "life liberty, and the pursuit of happiness"—was himself a slave-owner. [Thomas] Jefferson lived in a slave-owning society, one in which half of the non-slave population, the women, were not equal citizens. Yet for all its flaws, that society's saving grace was its foundation on a certain set of beliefs that transcended the individuals, their prejudices, and their times and allowed for the possibility of a different future, foreshadowing a time when other women and men, a Martin Luther King Jr. or an Elizabeth Cady Stanton, could take their ideas and words and suffuse them with new and risky and bold meanings, and with new dreams.[54]

These new meanings connect to the promise, if not the practice, of the Founding generation.

The second answer to the problem of inequality focuses on the (small *d*) democratic element of the Constitution. An elected government by and for "the People" marked a clear break from the hierarchical power of the monarchy in England. The establishment of democratic voting represented a move away from an aristocratic past, and toward equality of status. The creation of a President who could be impeached and voted out of office opened the door for citizen–politicians, not kings. Explicitly, the

Constitution abolished the trappings of privilege and hereditary status such as titles of nobility:

> *No title of nobility shall be granted by the United States.*
> *(Article I, Section 9)*

The rejection of unequal status made sense as many of the Framers came from humble backgrounds. Benjamin Franklin was the son of a candlemaker, and Roger Sherman (a Connecticut delegate) the son of a cobbler.[55] Equality, as a touchstone of political participation, became the foundation from which to build a more equal society. These developments, while unexceptional today, were radical experiments in a new type of egalitarian government.[56]

And to our credit, the country—through civil struggle and a civil war—took up this foundational challenge to unequal status and overcame it. To look at the Constitution today with the additions of the Thirteenth, Fourteenth, Fifteenth, Nineteenth, Twenty-Fourth, and Twenty-Six Amendments, you have a clear rejection of inequality. Collectively these Amendments forbid discrimination based on race, ancestry, sex, age, and economic status, and are a constitutional requirement of mutual respect. Even in the face of economic, social, and historical discrimination, the constitutional principle of equality reminds us of our fundamental sameness. Like the "Equal Justice Under Law" motto engraved on the facade of the United States Supreme Court building, equality is a constitutional aspiration.

Why Equality Matters
Seeing Equality

"The jury achieves symbolically what cannot be achieved practically—the presence of the entire populace at every trial."[57] When you vote in a presidential election, you cast your ballot as one of hundreds of millions. When you vote in a jury, you are one of twelve. Jury service thus allows you to see equality in action. In a world that is anything but equal, we tend to forget what equality feels like. You know your presidential vote counts as much as anyone else's, but you also know that the lobbyists, interest groups, media centers, and activists have more influence in the political process than your single vote. Economic and societal disparities also tend to undermine the belief that we are really equal. But in the jury room those differences become irrelevant. Your view of the facts is not any more persuasive because you are rich and famous. Your legal reasoning does not change just because you are poor. The principle of one person, one vote, is observable on jury duty. There is a leveling of status that is important to democracy.[58] This leveling mechanism strips away the divisions of our normal, unequal society.

All jurors start on an even playing field. You begin with the same sources and quantity of information. Unlike the rest of life, in which specialized knowledge or education can play a deciding role, on a jury you have a defined set of facts. Whether you are a rocket scientist or reporter, a linguist or laborer, jurors are given the same facts. Jurors see the same witnesses and hear the same arguments. The rules of decision require that the verdict must come from those facts. Thus no juror is more privileged or advantaged in thinking about the case. With equal information comes an equalized debate. Such equality is an uncommon experience, which is why the practice of participating in juries is so important.

A decision that begins with an equality of information allows for another principle of constitutional equality to flourish: the equality of ideas. In a jury room you have a space in which each voice is important, minority voices are protected, and each voice has a dignity that can shape the result.[59] Jurors thus begin seeing other citizens as equally valuable contributors. Jurors have commented to me that they were shocked at the level of respect given to one anothers' views. One foreman explained that he made sure to give each person exactly equal time throughout the deliberations because no person was more important than anyone else. No matter how you came into the jury room, because you are interpreting the same facts, you are required to listen to (and hopefully appreciate) the insights of others. This practice, then, spills outside the jury room.

Because lawyers cannot communicate with individual jurors during the actual trial, we spend a lot of time watching how jurors act in and out of the courtroom. And because we know only a bit of information about the jurors and are trying to intuit more, we tend to notice whom jurors hang out with and talk to, and what they do during their breaks. What you see, invariably, is an interaction that crosses normal societal boundaries. Jurors who would normally never speak with one another will share a sandwich day after day. Jurors get to talk to and interact with one another as equals—not as bosses, employees, or within some other societal power structure. People from all walks of life bond together as jurors.[60] A colleague of mine had a jury that bonded so much during a prolonged trial that they still regularly get together for dinner. This leveling develops mutual respect—a critical component of democracy.[61]

Diverse Perspectives

Trials involve the resolution of human conflict. Your jury experience may immerse you a world completely unfamiliar to your normal existence. I have had jurors joke that their jury experience had taught them more about "crack dens" then they had ever expected to know. The same can be said for product manufacturing claims, contract law, automobile crash reconstruction, or the interconnected family or gang conflicts that underlie many violent acts. To resolve these human disputes through law, we ask jurors to bring their diverse personal experiences and judgment to analyze the facts of each case.

Equality matters because it allows for different perspectives to be aired. Juries succeed because they bring varied points of view to bear on the evidence. As the Supreme Court once concluded, "[J]uries fairly chosen from different walks of life bring into the jury box a variety of different experiences, feelings, intuitions and habits. Such juries may reach completely different conclusions than would be reached by specialists in any single field."[62] To work as intended, then, a jury cannot have certain groups purposefully excluded or devalued.[63]

Jurors will often remark how they all approached the case with markedly different views and yet got to the same result. I once had both a former drug dealer (admitted in jury selection) and an administrative judge on my jury in a drug distribution case. Interestingly, they started out with different intuitions about the case—the former drug dealer was for conviction and the judicial officer for acquittal—but each came around to see the evidence in the same way. To watch these jurors (both African American men) explain their differing views to the other jurors (themselves from all sorts of racial and economic backgrounds) was to see diversity and equality in action.

Odd as it sounds, sometimes jurors are required to act as interpreters of human nature for other jurors who may not be familiar with the factual or cultural situation they are confronting. Kim Taylor-Thompson, a law professor and former trial lawyer, explains that occasionally people of one race or ethnic group must translate the reactions of a witness for jurors who may be simply unfamiliar with the situation:

The role of interpreter is not new to people of color in a mixed racial setting. The ability to bridge cultural gaps becomes critical in any effort to explain reactions or experiences that may be unfamiliar to—or at least uncommon for—members of dominant groups by virtue of their position in society. Particularly, when a trial involves issues of race or a person of color's reactions are at issue in a trial, a juror of color's perceptions may be critical to a determination of truth.[64]

Of course, it need not involve race or ethnicity. Sometimes experience with small business, or health ailments, or family dynamics, or any of a number of personal experiences will allow one juror to translate for other jurors. The point is that the diversity of juror experience enriches the work product of jury verdicts.

Such a conclusion is not just constitutional theory, but empirically based in fact. Two of the leading jury researchers in the United States, Neil Vidmar and Valerie P. Hans, studied the makeup of juries and resulting jury verdicts and concluded that a representative jury was better.[65] Simply put, the research shows that a diverse (meaning representative) jury took longer to deliberate, tended to discuss a wider range of issues, and on average was more accurate in understanding and evaluating the facts.[66] The different ways of looking at the evidence engendered more debate and discussion, and these collective insights resulted in more thoughtful outcomes. The studies concluded that diversity resulted in a more reasoned verdict.

All this is to show why courts focus on your right to serve on a jury. Equality in jury service and the protection against discrimination exists to allow you this opportunity to see equality in practice. It also provides legitimacy to the court system that all people are contributing to the administration of justice.

[Trial by jury] is the most transcendent privilege which any subject can enjoy or wish for, that he cannot be affected either in his property, his liberty, or his person, but by the unanimous consent of twelve of his neighbours and equals.
—William Blackstone

U.S. Court House and Post Office (n.d., ca. 1907) Completed in 1888
SUPERVISING ARCHITECT: Mifflin E. Bell
The United States District Court for the Northern District of Texas met here until 1930; the United States Circuit Court for the Northern District of Texas met here until that court was abolished in 1912. Razed in 1939.

SOURCE: NATIONAL ARCHIVES, RG 121-BS, BOX 84, FOLDER P, PRINT 1

4

Connecting to the Common Good

Thank You for Your Service

Jury selection ends with a hushed series of whispers. Then the trial judge intones those fateful words: "For those of you sitting in the jury box, you will be the jurors in this case. For the rest of you, thank you for your service, you may return to the jury office and tell them you have been excused." These words produce a wonderful array of human emotion. Looks of abject horror appear on the faces of those jurors caught unaware of the meaning of shuffling back and forth to the jury box. Looks of resignation come from those jurors who had already figured it out. Eyes roll. Lungs gasp in audible sighs. And then there are the smiles—broad smiles—on all the rest of the jury panel, relieved to have escaped jury service this time.

Contrast those reactions with the emotions at the end of the case. The next time the judge thanks the jurors "for their service," the trial is over. They are finished, having completed a process that has changed them, knowingly or unknowingly. To look at the expressions of jurors after the verdict, after the thanks, is to see the subtle changes that make jury service meaningful. There are almost always contented smiles, nods, and deep looks of satisfaction of a problem resolved but not completely settled. A thoughtfulness remains, as if the contested conversations swirling in the jury room have not yet quieted themselves.

The experiential arc between those two moments follows a well-worn path of common connection. The change from being a potential juror to becoming an actual jury member presents a shift in role. Jurors do not act alone. As a juror, you are not simply an individual sitting in judgment. A jury is not twelve individual judges, but a single judge made up of twelve decision makers. Jurors don't just participate, they participate together—like the motto on the Great Seal of the United States, "E pluribus unum" (out of many, one).[1] That moment then—when the judge says you've been selected—is transformative. It bonds jurors together, connecting them in a common purpose.

And what is this purpose for which you've been connected to your fellow citizens? You know there is a dispute—a contract, an injury, a crime. You know that it doesn't involve you personally. Because of the requirement of impartiality, whatever you are called on to decide will not directly affect you. The purpose is to come together to resolve a problem affecting the larger community. Jurors are required to look outward, to the problems of others, to the common good.

Public Virtue

Jury duty is not misnamed. The requirement to alter your normal routine, to come to an unfamiliar place, to show up day after day, to do so without commensurate pay,[2] and to face unexplained delays is a "duty." There is real sacrifice involved in answering this call and providing this service. I once had the pleasure of talking to a distinguished judge the afternoon she was called to jury duty. I asked her if she had been picked. Her response was "mercifully no." It was not that she did not understand the value of jury duty. She did. She had, in fact, served on three juries in her lifetime. As a judge she knew the importance of jurors to the legal system. Her response simply reflected that she had too much court work to do the next day. There were just too many cases, and too many people counting on her. It was too difficult to take on another duty.

But for those who founded this country, the difficulty was precisely the point. To sacrifice one's own interests for the common good defined the (small *r*) republican spirit.[3] The theory behind classical republicanism envisioned a government centered on active citizenship whereby individuals gave up private interests for the public good.[4] The Founders' republicanism focused on creating a government that encouraged the interplay of participation, deliberation, equality, and universalism to create a system directed toward the common good.[5] For revolutionaries creating a new nation, the ideal of a government that could foster a public good was a great selling point: "No phrase except 'liberty' was invoked more often by the Revolutionaries than 'the public good.'"[6] Thomas Paine defined republicanism as the good of the people, not the king: "The word *republic* means the *public good*, or the good of the whole, in contradistinction to the despotic form, which makes the good of the sovereign, or of one man, the only object of the government."[7] Striving for the public good was, thus, a part of our constitutional foundation.[8]

With the appeal to the public good came the sacrifice necessary by citizens to make it so. To create a public good you needed citizens instilled with "public virtue," who would knowingly fulfill their duty to the larger common purpose.[9] Acting with public virtue meant that in their capacity as political actors, citizens were expected to look to the greater interests of the community and not just their individual interests.[10] Essentially, the political philosophy behind the idea was that without a king to control the people, Americans had to rely on the virtue of private citizens who believed in prioritizing the nation over the individual.[11] Strands of this thinking are familiar to anyone who has sacrificed in the military, worked for the government, or served the public interest.

While historians may disagree as to whether the United States ever became the republican nation envisioned by those creating the new country (and whether we would even want that ideal), the spirit of republicanism is firmly lodged in the jury. As jurors, we sacrifice, we serve, and we exercise the power to control through collective action the principles of justice in our community.[12]

So, as you sit there counting the money you are not earning from your job, or the time you are missing with loved ones, just remember that your time on jury duty is a place to connect with the public virtue envisioned by the Constitution. Your personal sacrifice reinforces the bonds of political connection, of collective action, of engagement with the "constitutional good."

Common Good and the Constitution

Jurors are not the only members of society expected to sacrifice for the common good. Jury service is a microcosm of what the Constitution expects from citizens and states on a national scale. Looking at the constitutional text through the lens of common connection reveals the importance of this foundational principle.

The Theory of the Common Good

Like jury service, which unites individuals to resolve a dispute within a community, our Constitution was a document of common connection. It "united" the states of America for a common purpose. While the term "common good" does not appear in the Constitution, the document's very existence represents a collective agreement toward resolving the problems inherent in self-government. The full Preamble reads:

> *We the People of the United States, in order to form a more perfect union, establish justice, insure domestic tranquility, provide for the common defense, promote the general welfare, and secure the blessings of liberty to ourselves and our posterity, do ordain and establish this Constitution for the United States of America.*

This language—"a more perfect union" focused on the "general welfare," and "the common defense"—is a call to "our" common good. The Preamble thus sets out the common ideals of a country before providing the governing structure of how to protect those ideals.

While it is an oversimplification to say that the Constitution's mechanisms for electing representatives, providing for debate and deliberation, and promising a measure of equality means that republicanism triumphed, the republican spirit—the idea of prioritizing the good of the nation over individual interests—certainly did. The Constitution expressly promises a "republican form of government":

> *The United States shall guarantee to every state in this union a republican form of government, and shall protect each of them against invasion, and on application of the legislature, or of the executive (when the legislature cannot be convened), against domestic violence. (Article IV, Section 4)*

By this, James Madison envisioned a constitutional system that would create a deliberative space for elected officials so that they could realize the public interest independent of personal or partisan gain. In *Federalist* No. 10, Madison wrote that a republican system of representation would:

> refine and enlarge the public views, by passing them through the medium of a chosen body of citizens, whose wisdom may best discern the true interest of their country, and whose patriotism and love of justice will be least likely to sacrifice it to temporary or partial considerations. Under such a regulation, it may well happen that the public voice, pronounced by the representatives of the people, will be more consonant to the public good than if pronounced by the people themselves, convened for the purpose.

Again, while the arguments are fraught with historical counterpoints, the ideal was to create a federal government that would encourage a search for the common good.

Our Common Interests

Beyond the ideal of common interests, as a practical matter, our common government connects us. The Constitution legally connected thirteen states previously held together by a loose association under the Articles of Confederation. It also created an interconnected economic market centered on national interests.[13] We needed a national currency, a national economy, and a national tax collection system. In fact, one of the foremost concerns of the early American government was that there was no way to collect revenue to support a common defense or national government.[14] States also had begun printing their own money, thereby depreciating their currency, increasing debt and inflation, and creating general economic insecurity.[15] Compounding the problem, communication among the states was hampered by inadequate roads and postal systems, which prevented interstate economic growth. The result was that a young country faced a deteriorating social and economic future and the real threat of dissolution.[16] A nation that had won a war of independence did not have the internal connective strength to secure a common future.

The remedy was a national Constitution, one that prioritized national common interests. One of the peculiar things about the Constitution is that within a document meant to limit government, it provided very specific powers to the early federal government, including the authority to build post roads, coin money, organize bankruptcies, collect taxes, and provide for the common military defense:

> *The Congress shall have power to lay and collect taxes, duties, imposts and excises, to pay the debts and provide for the common defense and general welfare of the United States …*

> *To regulate commerce with foreign nations, and among the several states …*

> *To establish … uniform laws on the subject of bankruptcies throughout the United States; …*

> *To coin money, regulate the value thereof, and of foreign coin, and fix the standard of weights and measures; …*

> *To establish post offices and post roads …*

> *To make all laws which shall be necessary and proper for carrying into execution the foregoing powers, and all other powers vested by this Constitution in the government of the United States … (Article I, Section 8)*

Right there, written into the Constitution, is the foundation for our tax system and interstate communication.

The Framers put the post office and taxes in the Constitution before the freedom of speech or religion. Why? The point is not mere practicality, but connection—finding ways to promote the common good by creating a common market across the country.

This constitutional call for the common good is thus more than just symbolic connecting points on paper: it relates also to connecting points in real life. Just as jury service connects us to serve the common good of the community, the Constitution gives Congress the ability to serve the common good of our nation. We need those interstate roads to drive through the many states as much as we need the post office to deliver the birthday card to grandma. The constitutional framework grants Congress the power to regulate commerce, broadly defined. This reality has opened up federal involvement into many aspects of our daily lives directed toward the common good. While we may disagree on the level of involvement or role of the federal government in defining that common good, the debate begins with a common starting point—the Constitution.

Common Laws

One obvious manifestation of the common good is the common laws that bind us together. If you are on a jury in federal court, you will apply the same law no matter what state you're in. If you are on a state jury, the laws may be different, but all will be consistent with constitutional constraints. Further, each state must give "full faith and credit" to the decisions of other states (including jury verdicts):

> Full faith and credit shall be given in each state to the public acts, records, and judicial proceedings of every other state. (Article IV, Section 1)

This means that a constitutionally enforceable right in one state must be honored in every other state. While states can establish their own laws, and come to different opinions on particular legal issues, they must give respect to the decisions of other state courts.

Moreover, the federal Constitution is the "supreme" law of the land, trumping other conflicting laws. Even though we have state constitutions and state laws, plus city, town, and village ordinances, the United States Constitution supersedes these rules. Further, under Article VI, our elected officials, Senators, Representatives, state legislators, and all executive and judicial officeholders must swear an oath to support the *federal* Constitution:

> *This Constitution, and the laws of the United States which shall be made in pursuance thereof; and all treaties made, or which shall be made, under the authority of the United States, shall be the supreme law of the land …*

> *The Senators and Representatives before mentioned, and the members of the several state legislatures, and all executive and judicial officers, both of the United States and of the several states, shall be bound by oath or affirmation, to support this Constitution …*

Taken together, the Supremacy Clause and the Oath or Affirmation Clause requires public officials to support constitutional rulings as the controlling law of the land.[17] This double protection was necessary in response to the history of states not following through on their obligations under the Articles of Confederation.

It is also your obligation. As a juror, you embody the same allegiance to support and defend the Constitution. As can be seen, the idea of the "common good" helped structure the Constitution and link a nation. The question of course is, how or why should this principle be practiced on jury duty?

Why Connecting to the Common Good Matters
Social Capital

Justice Oliver Wendell Holmes once stated, "Taxes are what you pay for a civilized society."[18] He might have added jury duty, because there are not many other requirements to be a modern citizen. Even voting is voluntary.

The question remains: what benefit do jurors get for this irregular service to the courts? In 2000, Robert Putnam wrote *Bowling Alone: The Collapse and Revival of American Community*, a book studying the decline in civic engagement, social connections, and community involvement in modern America.[19] Putnam traced a downward shift in participation rates through all sorts of political, civic, and social activities in the last two decades of the twentieth century. For example, during that time Putnam found that people voted less, participated in politics less, and chose to run for office less often than in the past.[20] Similarly, civic participation rates dropped. People stopped joining civic organizations like the PTA[21] or the NAACP,[22] or even bowling leagues. Across the board, personal and social connections decreased as the American family lived a much more isolated existence.[23]

Putnam found that one significant consequence of this decline was the erosion of "social capital."[24] Like "economic capital" or "human capital," "social capital" involves the value of social networks.[25] Essentially, the theory of social capital is that connections among individuals increase the productivity of individuals and groups in the community.[26] According to Putnam, the benefits of social capital are many. Social capital allows neighbors to mediate community problems by creating

social understandings that help identify mutually benefi-
cial solutions.[27] Social networks foster trust and mutual
respect between people who interact on a regular basis.[28]
Social capital helps broaden awareness and empathy,
demonstrating how individuals in a community are tied
together, thus undermining prejudice or stereotypes.[29]
Social capital increases information flow, providing both
education and interpersonal development. After marshal-
ing a large volume of studies, statistics, and charts about
the value of social connections, Putnam made the simple but striking conclusion that "social capital makes us
smarter, healthier, safer, richer, and better able to govern
a just and stable democracy."[30]

Juries play only a passing role in Putnam's work. In
part, this is because Putman analyzed voluntary social
organizations, and, as we know, jury duty isn't voluntary.
Yet many of the benefits of social capital can be observed
in the jury. To look at the jury through the lens of social
capital, you see a very valuable commodity.

Jury service is a connecting institution. To enter a
room and confront complex moral judgments, or even
simple credibility contests, requires the development of
social skills that foster social capital. Through the process of deliberation, jurors are made aware of different viewpoints, sometimes even new worlds, as they are
asked to judge life choices, industries, and realities that
they may never have encountered before. Jurors must
learn to trust others, as they are required to share personal thoughts with strangers. Through jury instructions,
jurors necessarily inform themselves about the legal system and the legal rules at play. Throughout the trial process, jurors develop the social mores necessary for success
in other group activities. After all, if you can work with
twelve people to agree on a verdict, you might be able to
get your neighbors to organize to fix a problem in your
community. Of course, jury service does not require a

long-term connected relationship. Yet the social connections strengthened during jury service are the same types
that Putnam found were missing in larger society. Your
jury service fills in some of the missing participatory civic
activity in modern America. In short, the production of
social capital through jury service provides a good return
on your investment of time.

Constitutional Virtue

At its most idealistic, the public virtue of the Founders
involved a selfless sacrifice of the individual to the greater
good. Picture the heroic Nathan Hale's cry that he regrets
that he has but one life to give to his country.[31] However,
truthfully for jurors, the fact is that your public virtue is
imposed, not selfless (nor always idealistic). You have to
give up a few days for your country under penalty of law,
and the regrets are real.

Yet, despite the hard work and personal sacrifice, there
is redeeming value. If you look at the collective effort in
a courtroom, you can see that constitutional virtue come
alive. By "constitutional virtue," I mean seeing your public service as not only separate from your own personal
interests, but as really more important than your own
interests. To appreciate the role you play as a constitutional citizen, you must see your role as connected to
something grander than your daily life.

D. Graham Burnett served as a foreman for a murder
case in New York City. In his book on the experience, *A
Trial by Jury*, he detailed the deliberations and the unset-
tling emotional impact of the case. He talked about the
haunting effect the jury service had on him. In the epi-
logue to the book he explained:

> In the weeks that followed, I tried to return to my
> normal life. I started going back to my office at the
> humanities center . . . Still, things did not really feel

the same. Life had been weirdly sapped of its vitality and importance; my work seemed bizarre and insignificant.... [During deliberations] my whole being had been focused on a single problem; the solution exacted much, demanding my full intellectual and emotional ranges, extending these. It was a shared problem, a difficult problem, and a problem of considerable immediate consequence. It drew on all of me, and all of others, and we were bound by this. Life hands one few such episodes, and they are, in a way, gifts that go on costing.[32]

Burnett's description captures the unsettled looks of jurors as they are excused from jury service. It is the feeling of having been immersed in another world and required to meet the challenge of judgment.

I once had a jury deliberate for seven days in a homicide trial. It was an emotional case of self-defense involving a young man. The young man had been attacked by an intoxicated older man with tragic results. There was no happy ending, as the older man had lost his life. The question for the jury was would my client lose his liberty because of his actions. The stakes were high, as the jury had a choice between murder or acquittal by self-defense. The deliberations were anguished and agonizing, but eventually the jury acquitted. At the end of the case, the prosecutor and I went back to talk to the exhausted jury members. Before we could begin, the foreman asked to say a few words. He explained that he believed this jury had worked as hard as any jury could, and then he did something unexpected. He asked that we all hold hands and bow our heads in a moment of silence to recognize the loss to the community and the families involved. He then went on to talk about the emotional weight of the jury's verdict.

As I stood there, head bowed, holding hands with the jurors and the prosecutor whom I had just fought a difficult case against, I thought of this healing circle. Our silent prayer provided closure for the jury in its decision-making role, as well as closure for the jury's larger decision for the community. This circle, which included a place for the community, was the jury's way of repairing the tear in the social fabric.

Tocqueville termed this civic investment "a kind of magistracy" by which you redirect your attentions toward others to consider the problems of larger society:

> The jury teaches every man not to recoil before the responsibility of his own actions. . . . It invests each citizen with a kind of magistracy, it makes them all feel the duties which they are bound to discharge towards society, and the part which they take in the Government. By obliging men to turn their attention to affairs which are not exclusively their own, it rubs off that individual egotism which is the rust of society.[33]

Rubbing the rust off society is another way of saying that the practice of focusing on others opens you to the sense of shared community. Jurors look to the common good because jury service forces you to think about the common good.

Jury duty is a civic ritual. It is a rite of passage that allows society to reconstitute its constitutional ideals every business day. Like the Founding Fathers, who locked themselves in a room, put aside their individual differences, kept their deliberations secret, and came out with a common solution to a very important problem, your jury deliberations result in a singular, collective verdict.[34] The shift from "juror" to "jury" mirrors the sublimation of individual egos for the public good. It is public virtue in action.

This ritual creates constitutional actors. Day after day, jurors follow the same routines, recite the same incantations, observe the same symbols, and respect the same constitutional authority. To share in this tradition means you are part of a common constitutional system. By jointly applying constitutional values you ensure that they become common values. Whether you are transformed or merely connected to something bigger than yourself, jury duty remains a shared connecting point in a larger constitutional structure.

United States Custom House and Post Office (n.d., ca. 1933) Completed in 1877

SUPERVISING ARCHITECT: Alfred B. Mullett
Extension completed in 1933

SUPERVISING ARCHITECT OF EXTENSION: James A. Wetmore
Still in use by the United States District Court for the Eastern District of Michigan

SOURCE: NATIONAL ARCHIVES, RG 121-BS, BOX 48, FOLDER CC, PRINT 6772

5

Living Liberty

Liberty on Trial

For most people, "liberty" is not synonymous with jury duty. Jurors feel like their own liberty—the freedom to live their lives—has been taken by judicial force. You are summoned to court. Day after day, you are told when to arrive, when to leave, and even when you can go to the bathroom. You sit in a particular numbered seat. You watch what others produce for you to watch. The rules of court are decided for you, and though you are a central part of the trial process, you have little independent control.

As you watch the parade of witnesses controlled by lawyers, you will not likely be struck by the revolutionary freedom of the jury. As you show up each morning, as you eat courthouse lunches every afternoon, you will not likely see the spirit of liberty in your surroundings.[1] Yet historically, the jury trial has been considered the great preserver of liberty in the United States.[2]

In colonial times, juries were hailed as the bulwark of liberty:[3] "On many occasions, fully known to the Founders of this country, jurors—plain people—have manfully stood up in defense of liberty against the importunities of judges and despite prevailing hysteria and prejudices."[4] At the time of the Founding, juries existed as one of the few local, decentralized, and public sources of power to check the controlling government—be it royal, federal, or state. Jury trials interposed ordinary citizens between judicial officials and the power of the law. Given the history of British tyranny and American rebellion through colonial juries, it should be no surprise that juries became synonymous with the protection of personal freedom and property. As James Madison stated, trial by jury "is as essential to secure the liberty of the people as any one of the pre-existent rights of nature."[5] This ennobling vision of the jury as protector of liberty fit within the larger constitutional aspiration of ensuring a governing structure that protected "the people." Madison distinguished the United States Constitution from its English counterpart by describing the English version as a "charter . . . of liberty . . . granted by power," and the American model as a "charter . . . of power . . . granted by liberty."[6] By this, Madison meant that the source of liberty derives from the people, not from the government.

As mentioned earlier, juries were so connected with liberty that a perceived lack of civil juries in the original text of the Constitution almost undermined the new government.[7] Strikingly, during the four months of the Constitutional Convention, the Founders discussed civil juries only twice,[8] and quickly decided against including a civil jury right in the text.[9] The public reaction to this omission was swift and furious.[10] Anti-Federalist authors, using pseudonyms such as "Centinel," "Brutus," and "Federal Farmer," launched criticisms of the new Constitution, voicing concern over the lack of civil jury protections as proof of the tyrannical intentions of the new federal government.[11]

This debate over the role of juries threatened to derail the national experiment. At least seven states ratifying the Constitution demanded an immediate amendment that included the protection of the civil jury trial.[12] In response, Alexander Hamilton wrote *Federalist* No. 83, to assure citizens that civil juries were not purposely excluded and were very much recognized as "a valuable safeguard to liberty."[13] The Anti-Federalists' call to liberty won the day. The inclusion of the right to a civil jury trial in the Seventh Amendment, as well as the criminal jury trial protections in the Sixth Amendment, represented the triumph of liberty concerns in a young nation.[14]

From this early history, jurors have remained a force to protect the liberty interests of the parties in court. In civil trials, be it against state government or private parties, the jury acts to protect consumers, contracting parties, property interests, and constitutional rights.[15] In criminal trials, the jury literally determines the liberty of the accused. In each case, the concept of liberty animates the same jury process many feel so constraining as they sit on jury duty.

Liberty and the Constitution
Enlightenment

More than any other Enlightenment principle that inspired our forefathers, "liberty" was the concept that united America. The Declaration of Independence recognizes the inalienable right to "life, liberty, and the pursuit of happiness." The Preamble to the Constitution promises to "secure the blessings of liberty to ourselves and our posterity." The Bill of Rights exists as a document of "negative liberties," reserving to the people their preexisting rights and circumscribing the powers of the federal government. In a young nation of free thinkers, revolutionaries, and religious dissenters, the right to be free from government control had strong appeal. "Give me liberty or give me death" was the rallying cry of the "Sons of Liberty" who fought and won the American Revolution.[16] President George Washington, having won a war and ruled a nation as its first President, bid farewell in 1796 with a call to a citizenry that valued a "love of liberty."[17] Since then, generations of American dreams have begun by passing under the torch of the Statue of Liberty, just as generations of American children have begun their day with the words "with liberty and justice for all" as part of the Pledge of Allegiance. The concept of a nation committed to liberty and a government protecting liberty is woven into the American identity. But what is American liberty? That is a question with almost too many answers. As the historian Forrest McDonald has observed:

> [I]t is no great exaggeration to say that for two decades prior to the meeting of the Constitutional Convention, American political discourse was an ongoing public forum on the meaning of liberty. And there was a wide range of opinion: almost the only thing generally agreed upon was that everybody wanted it. Everything else—what liberty was, who deserved it, how much of it was desirable, how it was obtained, how it was secured—was subject to debate.[18]

And it is a debate that continues to the present day, as politicians and citizens contest the role of government and the need for liberty in a society that must balance social order and personal freedom.

Sitting in court you are part of that ongoing debate about the ideal of liberty. When a lawyer steps out into the well of the court, there is no spotlight. Yet the courtroom has been a stage for some of the most dramatic tests of freedom in our history. Famous Supreme Court cases involving the First Amendment started out as criminal prosecutions for sedition, anarchy, and incitement against the government.[19] Famous religious freedom cases started out as criminal prosecutions for nontraditional religious expression.[20] The daily reality of famous and even not so famous criminal cases is a test of the social order.

But it must be remembered that in many of those famous cases, the jury (and judges) actually failed to protect liberty. The ideals failed to overcome the reality. The community sentiment against unpopular minority views triumphed and resulted in convictions that the Supreme Court would later overturn. Jury verdicts restricted free speech. Religious practice was criminalized. Prejudice won the case. Certainly, as a trial lawyer, when I stepped out into that well of the courtroom, I was mindful that the twelve strangers looking back might well lack the moral courage to make the hard decisions required. Acquittal or conviction demands courage. Yet, while I stood there and looked face to face with each juror, I realized that the stage was not for me. It was for them—for the real actors in the play—the constitutional actors of the jury. The constitutional structure vests the jury with the ultimate decision to balance liberty with community order.

The Structure of Liberty

Part of that decision is guided by the Constitution itself, which is a document of enumerated powers. Its structured purpose is to define the limits of the federal government, reserving all other power to the people and the states. In limiting federal power from infringing on the freedom of the people, the words "no" or "not" appear dozens of times in the Constitution and dozens more times in the Bill of Rights.[21] In between the "no's" rests the liberty of a nation.

The structural protection of liberty rests on the creation of a tripartite system of government with Legislative, Executive, and Judicial Branches. The division between each branch of federal government prevents the centralization of power. The further division of power between state and local governments diffuses any concentration of power from the federal center. Regular elections, direct voting, juries, and the guarantee of a "republican form of government" all create a check on the power of the federal government. Similarly, an independent judiciary with a Supreme Court that can interpret and declare what the law means, provides opportunities for individuals to challenge infringements on their rights.[22]

In addition to structural liberty protections, the Constitution in Article I, Section 9, explicitly prohibits Congress from having overreaching power against individuals. It forbids religious tests for public office, guarantees open political debate, and creates a narrow definition of treason.[23] And it guarantees the right to habeas corpus and criminal trials for individuals who might run afoul of the government.[24]

In 1791, the Bill of Rights continued the tradition of protecting civil and personal liberty. Point by point, right by right, the first ten Amendments articulated the Founding principles of liberty. Liberty of conscience is enshrined in the Religious Freedom Clauses, just as liberty of thought finds sanctuary in the First Amendment's protection of expression, the press, assembly, and the ability to petition the government for change.[25]

The Second Amendment guarantees the right to bear arms and establish a militia to act as a counterweight to any centralized federal army.

The Third Amendment protects us from having troops quartered in our homes, thus ensuring that a standing army cannot be used to intimidate citizens during peacetime.[26]

The Fourth Amendment protects against unreasonable searches and seizures, and requires a warrant from a detached judicial magistrate. Expanding outward from the safety of ourselves and our families, the Fourth Amendment encompasses a reasonable expectation of privacy free from government intrusion.

The Fifth Amendment protects persons from unfounded criminal proceedings by requiring present-ment to a grand jury before a criminal trial can begin. It protects persons through the Double Jeopardy Clause. It forbids self-incrimination. It protects against unwar-ranted deprivation of property through the Takings Clause.

The Sixth and Seventh Amendment interpose juries and other trial rights to protect individual rights from state control.

The Eighth Amendment protects against "cruel and unusual punishments" as well as excessive bail or fines for those at the mercy of government police power.

The Ninth Amendment reserves all un-enumerated rights to the people. Even the structure of federalism in the Tenth Amendment is an effort to protect state and individual autonomy from an overreaching federal government:

The Bill of Rights

Congress shall make no law respecting an establishment of religion, or prohibiting the free exercise thereof; or abridging the freedom of speech, or of the press; or the right of the people peaceably to assemble, and to petition the government for a redress of grievances. (First Amendment)

A well regulated militia, being necessary to the security of a free state, the right of the people to keep and bear arms, shall not be infringed. (Second Amendment)

No soldier shall, in time of peace be quartered in any house, without the consent of the owner, nor in time of war, but in a manner to be prescribed by law. (Third Amendment)

The right of the people to be secure in their persons, houses, papers, and effects, against unreasonable searches and seizures, shall not be violated, and no warrants shall issue, but upon probable cause, supported by oath or affirmation, and particularly describing the place to be searched, and the persons or things to be seized. (Fourth Amendment)

No person shall be held to answer for a capital, or otherwise infamous crime, unless on a presentment or indictment of a grand jury, except in cases arising in the land or naval forces, or in the militia, when in actual service in time of war or public danger; nor shall any person be subject for the same offense to be twice put in jeopardy of life or limb; nor shall be compelled in any criminal case to be a witness against himself, nor be deprived of life, liberty, or property, without due process of law; nor shall private property be taken for public use, without just compensation. (Fifth Amendment)

In all criminal prosecutions, the accused shall enjoy the right to a speedy and public trial, by an impartial jury of the state and district wherein the crime shall have been committed, which district shall have been previously ascertained by law, and to be informed of the nature and cause of the accusation; to be confronted with the witnesses against him; to have compulsory process for obtaining witnesses in his favor, and to have the assistance of counsel for his defense. (Sixth Amendment)

In suits at common law, where the value in controversy shall exceed twenty dollars, the right of trial by jury shall be preserved, and no fact tried by a jury, shall be otherwise re-examined in any court of the United States, than according to the rules of the common law. (Seventh Amendment)

Excessive bail shall not be required, nor excessive fines imposed, nor cruel and unusual punishments inflicted. (Eighth Amendment)

The enumeration in the Constitution, of certain rights, shall not be construed to deny or disparage others retained by the people. (Ninth Amendment)

The powers not delegated to the United States by the Constitution, nor prohibited by it to the states, are reserved to the states respectively, or to the people. (Tenth Amendment)

In sum, the Bill of Rights is a charter of individual liberty: "The very purpose of the Bill of Rights was to withdraw certain subjects from the vicissitudes of political controversy, to place them beyond the reach of majorities and officials and to establish them as legal principles to be applied by the courts. One's right to life, liberty and property, to free speech, a free press, freedom of worship and assembly, and other fundamental rights may not be submitted to vote; they depend on the outcomes of no elections."[27] While initially applying only to the federal government, most of these rights were incorporated into the states through the Fourteenth Amendment.

Further constitutional Amendments continued to expand and protect the liberty interests of Americans. The Thirteenth Amendment ended slavery. The Fifteenth, Nineteenth, Twenty-Fourth, and Twenty-Sixth Amendments expanded voting rights. The Fourteenth Amendment's "life, liberty, or property" due process protection echoed the Fifth Amendment and established procedural protections against the states. In its totality, liberty protections were assured by a series of overlapping protections in the structure and text of the Constitution.

Why Liberty Matters
Autonomy Cost

Liberty, like any precious commodity, has a cost. Certainly, the Founding Fathers who risked their lives in a war with the British Empire recognized the cost. The jury system, like the larger legal system, is not always convenient or efficient. It, too, has a cost. To quote Thomas Paine, "Those who expect to reap the benefits of freedom, must, like men, undergo the fatigue of supporting it."[28]

If you think about a long criminal trial, tens of thousands, sometimes millions of dollars are expended. The collective hours of jurors, judges, clerks, marshals, and lawyers result in a huge outlay of time and expense. And all of it happens around a single individual—sometimes a despised and hated individual. Similarly, an individual lawsuit directed against the government or a corporation can cost millions and millions of dollars. One child damaged by a negligent agency, one family maimed by a defective product, and the result can be decades in court. Yet the entire legal system exists because of a goal of respecting the autonomy—the worth—of the single individual. From a cost-benefit perspective, it may not make economic sense, so you have to wonder why we do it.

The answer lies in a value beyond efficiency. One of the most uplifting and yet surprising observations comes from watching juries handling true "dead loser" cases. As a defense lawyer, there have been some cases (not many) in which the formality of trial was more of a formality than most. Not that I didn't try hard, not that I didn't poke holes in the government's evidence, but the facts were the facts. And the facts were really bad. Going back and talking to juries after those cases, when damning evidence has been presented and yet the jury took days to sift through everything and make sure that they had reached the right result, was always inspiring. Jurors could have reached the result in minutes, yet they took days to make sure a person's liberty was protected.

All of the time-consuming constitutional protections speak to something deeper about the choices we have made to signify "our respect for the accused as a human being."[29] Any infringement on these protections or the jury's power to protect the individual is treated very seriously. As Justice Antonin Scalia commented in a criminal appeal:

> [O]ur decision cannot turn on whether or to what degree trial by jury impairs the efficiency or fairness of criminal justice. One can certainly argue that both these values would be better served by leaving justice entirely in the hands of professionals. . . . There is not one shred of doubt, however, about the Framers' paradigm for criminal justice: not the civil-law ideal of administrative perfection, but the common-law ideal of limited state power accompanied by strict division of authority between judge and jury. . . . The Framers would not have thought it too much to demand that, before depriving a man of . . . his liberty, the State should suffer the modest inconvenience of submitting its accusations to the unanimous suffrage of twelve of his equals and neighbors.[30]

From the perspective of the "accused," a jury trial provokes both awe and fear. Imagine the sense of unease that results when sixty or more citizens file in and fill the courtroom for your jury selection. They stare at you. They are here for you. Many times my clients were struck by the sheer number of people called to hear their case: "All of these people are here for me?" And then, during the days or weeks of trial, you know that you have imposed on the time and attention of these twelve citizens every day. At the same time, you are depending on those same people to make the most important decision imaginable. For people unused to such attention, this intense focus is hard to comprehend. But the focus, attention, and modest inconvenience exist because we want this protective filter when the stakes of making a mistake are so high.[31]

Similarly, the right of an individual to challenge a "wrong" through the civil legal system is a form of liberty protection. Civil rights lawsuits to remedy statutory or constitutional violations serve to check the power of government. Across a vast spectrum of legal issues, these cases depend on juries to determine the reasonableness of official conduct.[32] Government benefits, police abuse, and negligence cases are all tried before juries. These lawsuits touch on almost every aspect of government's relationship with the citizenry.[33] Again, the role of an independent judiciary set up to hear these kinds of lawsuits recognizes the value we place in challenging government action (or inaction). And while it is certainly not easy, the jurors who listen and decide these individual complaints show the greatest sort of constitutional respect to the individual.

Rules of Liberty

In the same way juries are required to find the facts, juries are required to follow the law. One of the things you agree to as a juror is that you will apply the law as explained by the judge. During every trial, the judge explains the controlling law of the case through jury instructions. Formal rules might not intuitively seem to be connected with the principle of liberty. We associate "liberty" with freedom, not rules. But American liberty is more connected with law than lawlessness. American liberty requires rules. To be allowed the political freedom to think, say, and do as you like, does not actually mean that you can do whatever you like. We believe in the freedom of political candidates to campaign, but that does not mean that candidates can threaten, silence, and intimidate the other candidates. We believe that everyone has the right to obtain property, but that does not mean that we permit people to steal other people's property.

In order to have liberty you must develop a government of laws. In what must be considered the singular expression of American liberty, the Declaration of Independence declared not simply a promise of liberty but the creation of a government to protect that liberty: "[T]o secure these rights, Governments are instituted among Men, deriving their just powers from the consent of the governed."[34] Liberty arises not in the absence of government but through the establishment of a representative system of government. A jury makes that Founding principle a reality, by instituting a democratically inspired process to protect individual rights.

Liberty and the rule of law are historically and textually connected in the Constitution. The term "liberty" makes two appearances in the Amendments under the Due Process Clause (no person shall be deprived "of life, liberty, or property, without due process of law"). Under the common law in effect at the time of the drafting of the Constitution, "due process" was limited to the technical and procedural mechanisms at trial. In other words, the rules of trial. As Alexander Hamilton wrote, "The words 'due process' have a precise technical import and are only applicable to the process and proceedings of the courts of justice."[35] A hundred years later, Hamilton's definition was quoted in the debates over the passage of the Fourteenth Amendment, which adopted the same due process language protecting "life, liberty, or property" in the states.[36] In other words, the original understanding of liberty was intertwined with rules of procedure.

This limited common law definition has since been expanded to incorporate a substantive component of due process predicated on a broader definition of personal liberty. Due process protections now cover a wide range of personal freedoms. As the Supreme Court stated in 1923:

> While this court has not attempted to define with exactness the liberty thus guaranteed, the term has received much consideration and some of the included things have been definitely stated. Without doubt, it denotes not merely freedom from bodily restraint but also the right of the individual to contract, to engage in any of the common occupations of life, to acquire useful knowledge, to marry, establish a home and bring up children, to worship God according to the dictates of his own conscience, and generally to enjoy those privileges long recognized at common law as essential to the orderly pursuit of happiness by free men.[37]

While interpretive issues remain concerning the extent of due process protections, your jury service remains one aspect of this practical connection between the rule of law and liberty. As a juror you are part of the government design to apply the law.

A juror's approach to jury instructions provides the most obvious reality of that application. You have to figure out the rules. The instructions are the carefully worded result of lawyers, judges, and scholars thinking about the law. For most jurors, untutored in the law, it may take several readings of the jury instructions to understand them. I have talked to jurors who explained that they took turns reading each instruction aloud to the group, considering every word. I have spoken to other jurors who literally diagramed the jury instructions as we were once taught in grammar class (I didn't ask any follow-up questions, having forgotten all about how to diagram sentences). And I saw one jury room that looked like it had been taken over by a graduate level English seminar. Notes, questions, and quotations were taped up on every square inch of wall with arrows, underlined words, and entire jury instructions rewritten in large text.

Many times jurors will ask the court and lawyers for clarification of a word or phrase. Numerous studies have shown that the problem with allowing lawyers and judges to write jury instructions is that lawyers and judges occasionally forget to talk like regular people.[38] While there has been some movement in a few jurisdictions to modify jury instructions into "plain language,"[39] in most cases the legal concepts are difficult and applying the law to the facts requires real effort. This is why we believe that juries are so critical to the process. In processing the facts and the law, you are giving the parties what they are due. This due process ensures that the rules are applied in a just manner. And if the system works as it should, the result is that the rules of law support the rule of law, which in turn protects all of us living within the rules of society.

Active Liberty

Jury trials play out in public. Witnesses come into court, they introduce themselves, spell their names, explain their background, and then detail what they saw, did, or experienced. They are then questioned about the accuracy, believability, or bias behind their testimony, and sent on their way. Physical evidence—the murder weapon or disputed contract—is introduced to bolster the testimony of the witnesses. A case can turn on a single statement or a single document.

Yet the hard work jurors do is not in the production of evidence, but in the processing of that evidence. The hard work happens in the jury box, where you must evaluate the information presented. Juries are active engines of information processing. While all an observer might see is you scribbling on your notepad, the entire show means nothing if you are not engaged in sorting through the information. In every trial there are two sides to the story. The choice of how to interpret the diverging versions comes down to the active engagement of the jury.

Like a computer synthesizing bits of data, jurors must formulate the information in a way that allows them to analyze it. Like someone struggling to fit the pieces of a puzzle together, the jury needs clues from the lawyers. The analysis that goes on in each juror's head is the key to a jury trial.

In most trials, the lawyers try desperately to figure out how jurors are processing the information. Lawyers study body language, note taking, and nonverbal clues to see the impact of their questions. A good lawyer must be able both to present the evidence and at the same time watch how the evidence is affecting particular jurors. In closing argument, the hope is to go back and emphasize the points that seemed to resonate. Of course, some jurors refuse to make eye contact with the lawyers. Some will nod at everything you say (making you feel really good until you notice they are also nodding at everything the other lawyer says as well). Some will write down detailed notes during the most meaningless part of the trial. And you know things are going badly when a juror appears to be nodding off, or sighing loudly at your questions. The point is that a jury trial involves an interactive but indirect process of communication. We are having an important conversation even if you cannot talk back.

Viewing the jury as an active, engaged body of thinkers is central to the liberty-protecting role we have created for the institution. While we generally define "liberty" as the freedom from government interference, liberty is rightly considered in broader terms. The work of jurors, acting as citizen–thinkers engaged in a conversation at trial, represents a form of liberty.

In his book *Active Liberty*, Supreme Court Justice Stephen Breyer addresses the issue of this democratic conception of American liberty: "The United States is a nation built upon principles of liberty. That liberty means not only freedom from government coercion *but also the freedom to participate in the government itself.*[40] In other words, "liberty" involves participation in the democratic process. "Active liberty" is a collective power. As Justice Breyer describes this broader vision of liberty:

> The concept of active liberty . . . refers to a sharing of a nation's sovereign authority among its people. Sovereignty involves the legitimacy of a governmental action. And a sharing of sovereign authority suggests several kinds of connection between that legitimacy and the people.
>
> For one thing, it should be possible to trace without much difficulty a line of authority for making of governmental decisions back to the people themselves. . . . And this authority must be broad. The people must have room to decide and leeway to make mistakes.
>
> For another, the people themselves should participate in government—though their participation may vary in degree. Participation is most forceful when it is direct, involving, for example, voting, town meetings, political party membership, or issue- or interest-related activities. It is weak, but still minimally exists, to the extent that it is vicarious, reflected, say, in the understanding that each individual belongs to the political community with the right to participate should he or she chose to do so.
>
> Finally, the people, and their representatives, must have the capacity to exercise their democratic responsibilities. They should possess the tools, such as information and education, necessary to participate and to govern effectively.
>
> When I refer to active liberty, I mean to suggest connections of this kind between the people and their government—connections that involve responsibility, participation, and capacity. Moreover, active liberty

cannot be understood in a vacuum, for it operates in the real world. And in the real world, institutions and methods of interpretation must be designed in a way such that this form of liberty is both sustainable over time and capable of translating the people's will into sound policies.[41]

Justice Breyer uses the theme of active liberty to discuss an interpretive method for deciding Supreme Court cases and controversies. Essentially, by looking to see what outcomes further this principle of collective participation in democracy, justices can make hard choices in particular cases. Active liberty involves a method of legal interpretation and analysis that "helps a community of individuals democratically find practical solutions to important contemporary social problems."[42]

Justice Breyer concentrates on judicial interpretation—how judges should think about the Constitution—and he does not analyze juries as an example of active liberty. Yet a jury certainly fits the theme. A jury "helps a community of individuals democratically find practical solutions to important contemporary social problems." Juries directly connect governmental decisions back to the people themselves. Jurors encourage participation in a democratic form. And jurors are taught the information necessary for a real-world practice of a democracy.

Considering juries as a manifestation of active liberty only recognizes the work jurors do in synthesizing information. Finding the facts by watching the witnesses and sifting through the evidence requires full engagement in the case. Even though you aren't allowed to get up from your seat, your participation changes the trial to a dynamic process. In doing this difficult work of finding practical solutions to social problems, juries strengthen this broad conception of active, American liberty.

You don't even have to be in court to see it. Three blocks from the courthouse in which I practiced stands the National Archives, perhaps the greatest collection of political ideas in the country. Its majestic stone walls entomb documents that guide a nation. During one particularly agonizing jury trial, and unable to face my colleagues back at work, I entered the calming air of the Archives' rotunda. Glass cases along a marble wall displayed the Charters of Freedom—the Declaration of Independence, the Constitution, and the Bill of Rights. Dozens of children filed past the documents. One older gentleman held up the procession as he carefully examined the document that founded a country. I made my way toward him. I leaned over his shoulder to read the faint black lines in the Bill of Rights. I squinted in the darkened room to see if there was some answer to my trial angst, some reaffirmation in those words. I could barely read the faded parchment. It seemed odd that everything I had been doing, my job, the jury's existence, each made real by the Sixth Amendment, were formalized into a document I could barely read. I wondered how we had translated those words into the reality of the criminal courtroom down the street.

As I was nudged aside by a crowd of expectant faces peering into the glass, I saw the answer. Those people who had come to see their history were the translators. Each one was a potential juror, potential voter, and active citizen. There was no revelation in the parchment, but only in the reflected glass. Those faces, those citizens, had to make the words real through practice. They were in the Archives that day absorbing the inspiration for the real-world practice of democracy. Beneath the exhibition of paintings titled "A New World Is at Hand," citizens saw that they belonged to a participatory political community, just like the jurors in my case. They were there to learn. They were there to participate. It was active liberty on display.

The very object of the jury system is to secure unanimity by a comparison of views, and by arguments among the jurors themselves.

—*Allen v. United States*, 164 U.S. 492, 501 (1896)

United States Post Office and Court House (n.d., ca. 1910) Completed in 1890
SUPERVISING ARCHITECT: Will. A. Freret
The United States District Court for the District of Kansas met here until 1932; the United States Circuit Court for the District of Kansas met here until that court was abolished in 1912. Razed in 1937.

SOURCE: NATIONAL ARCHIVES, RG 121-C, BOX 12, FOLDER H, PRINT 20

6

Deciding Through Deliberation

Deciding to Decide

So, it is time to decide. The trial is over. The evidence is completed. You and your fellow jurors sit around a table. You have been asked to make the final decision in a case. You are about to begin the process of jury deliberations. You are about to practice the principle of deliberation.

One of the most puzzling things for jurors is that once inside the jury room there is no guidebook on how to decide.[1] Sure you have the jury instructions, with the burdens of proof, standards of proof, elements of charges, and ways of judging the different types of evidence. But while the jury instructions can help you think through the evidence, they do not instruct you on how to decide. There is no set process on how the jury should make its decision. All you are told is to "deliberate."

What is deliberation? Deliberation involves collective decision making—a willingness to think together using reason and informed discussion to come to a final decision. It is in jury deliberations that a jury thinks.

Why is deliberation important? Because the process of deliberating—of sitting down and hashing out a problem with others—creates better thinkers and better decisions. As thinkers you become invested, informed, and connected. Such dynamic thinking forces you to consider different ideas and reason your way to a final decision. It offers a personal and legitimate way to resolve conflict. Practically, it means that twelve individuals with twelve different observations, intuitions, and judgments must be fit into one verdict.

How are jurors supposed to approach deliberation? Again, there is no set way, leaving the method to the creativity and inspiration of the jurors. Typically, however, jurors approach deliberations using either a "verdict-driven" method or an "evidence-driven" method.[2] A verdict-driven method involves an initial vote, after which jurors align themselves with the differing sides and talk about the evidence that supports either side. An evidence-driven method means that jurors go through and discuss the evidence and witnesses without any formal vote counting.[3] The difference in the evidence-driven model is that "[r]ather than offer only the facts supportive of their preferred verdict, jurors tend to talk about all of the evidence as they collectively aim to develop a common story of the events."[4]

According to studies done on both methods, "[t]he verdict-driven style tends to be faster but also is more likely to lead to a situation in which the jurors cannot agree on a final decision."[5] People become more polarized more quickly, as positions harden during the debate.[6] In fact, some jury instructions caution jurors to approach their initial discussions with civility and delicacy so as not to harden positions out of ego or personal investment. No matter the approach, deliberation is common in all successful jury discussions.

One juror summarized their deliberations as follows: We all went around the room and gave our opinion of the evidence. We talked and talked about the various arguments. Some people were convinced of guilt, some unsure. Then we all went around the room again. This time there were more questions. The conversation evolved, asking more and more questions. We went around the third time, with even more questions. Soon, everyone had more questions than answers. It took a long conversation after that, but we realized we knew our decision. Then we talked some more.

The Power of Twelve

In a traditional jury, you are one of twelve other citizens. The idea of twelve people sitting in judgment dates back to the twelfth century. Under the reign of Henry II, the sheriff could swear twelve men to give a verdict on land disputes.[7] In the middle of the fifteenth century, twelve jurors began hearing evidence in courts of law.[8] The historic justification for the number twelve is contested. Some believe it derived from the twelve apostles or the twelve Tribes of Israel or any of the other things that come in groups of twelve.[9]

A jury of twelve was duly imported to America. With only very limited exception in the colonies, twelve remained the set number for juries.[10] As the Supreme Court stated in 1898, "The wise men who framed the Constitution of the United States and the people who approved it were of [the] opinion that life and liberty, when involved in criminal prosecutions, would not be adequately secured except through the unanimous verdict of twelve jurors."[11] This understanding was consistent with the early jury practice before and after the framing of the Constitution.

Abruptly, in 1970—and after six hundred years in England and America—the Supreme Court changed this requirement of twelve jurors. In a still debatable opinion, the Court allowed for the experimentation of juries with less than twelve persons.[12] Ostensibly, the justification for the change involved a desire to make jury service less onerous on citizens.[13] Smaller juries meant fewer potential jurors to call to the courthouse. In *Williams v. Florida*, the Court termed the twelve-person requirement an "accident of history" and could find no constitutional basis for requiring a number whose selection appeared to "rest on little more than mystical or superstitious insights into the significance of 12."[14] In reaching this conclusion, the Supreme Court ignored any consideration of the effectiveness of juries of less than twelve people, simply deciding that there was no constitutional requirement for the requirement of twelve jurors.

Since *Williams* was decided, numerous scholars have questioned the Supreme Court's decision on empirical (and historical) grounds, demonstrating that smaller juries have a negative effect on deliberations.[15] Specifically, scholars who study jury dynamics (in real trials and in mock jury experiments) have determined that smaller juries are more unpredictable.[16] In civil cases, if you compare jury damage awards to a community average, two-thirds of twelve-person juries match the community average (meaning the damage awards were in line with the norm), but only half of six-person juries match the average.[17] This means that the damage awards from six-person juries will swing more wildly up or down in unpredictable ways. Apparently, the reason for this difference is that smaller juries are more easily swayed by one vocal position (one dominant personality), leading to more uncertain damages outcomes across the board.

Similarly, the cross-sectional ideal of jury representation suffers as a result of smaller juries. In simple terms, a reduced jury size decreases the chances that a jury represents the full diversity of a community. Or as one scholar reasoned, "If we draw juries at random from a population consisting of 90 percent of one kind of person and 10 percent another kind of person (categorized by politics, race, religion, social class, wealth, or whatever), 72 percent of juries of size 12 will contain at least one member of the minority group, compared to only 47 percent of juries of size six."[18] While the same proportion of people from the minority group will serve on juries in general, they will be over- or underrepresented on particular juries.

Finally, studies have shown that a smaller jury may affect the process of deliberation.[19] Within a smaller group, individuals may contribute less or be more easily swayed by the biases or judgments of others.[20] One of the most consistent findings is that individual jurors are more likely to compromise when isolated in their decision. Thus the difference between a 5–1 vote split and a 10–2 vote split is not equivalent. The two dissenting voices in the 10–2 situation are more likely to convince others (or at least prolong the discussion) than is the individual in the 5–1 situation.[21] Simply by having another person on your side gives you more confidence to hold on to a minority position.

The above studies were validated somewhat by the Supreme Court in 1978 in a case that drew the line at juries of less than six people, holding that those minijuries violated the Constitution.[22] Currently, all but four states require juries of twelve persons for felony criminal cases. Eighteen states allow fewer than twelve jurors for general jurisdiction civil trials.[23] Federal felony trials require twelve jurors. Federal civil trials require between six to twelve jurors.[24]

Whatever the merits to the arguments over the size of the jury, the one thing that has remained clear is that a jury must deliberate.[25] Be it six people or twelve people or somewhere in between, the process of deliberation is critical to the decision. At a minimum, the Constitution mandates a jury of "sufficient size to promote group deliberation, to insulate members from outside intimidation, and to provide a representative cross-section of the community."[26]

Deliberation represents a very American way of deciding something.[27] There is an element of democratic structure to the voting, there is a presumption of equality, and there is a coming together to decide that mirrors the voting process for elections. It should be no surprise then to see how this principle shaped our constitutional founding.

Deliberation and the Constitution
A Deliberative Founding

More than any document in American history, the Constitution was a deliberative act. In the summer of 1787, fifty-five men debated the ideas that became the ideological foundation of a country. While many of these men were well-known political leaders—George Washington, Benjamin Franklin, Alexander Hamilton, and James Madison—they approached the creation of a Constitution with opposing views. Two of the New York representatives left days after arriving because of their opposition to the idea of a new Constitution.[28] From May 25 to September 17, the remaining Founding Fathers debated issues of state power, voting rights, taxes, liberty, and structural protections, and other foundational concerns.[29] Madison recorded the passionate discussions and arguments of each participant. The Constitutional Convention involved four months of sustained daily debate about the structure of the future government.[30] The Founders were talking and thinking, all together in a room. Then it was decided—like a jury verdict, a sustained discussion resulted in a final decision. As the constitutional text concluded:

> *Done in convention by the unanimous consent of the states*
> *present ... (Article VII)*

It was a unified act of national deliberation.

The Founders' initial discussions spilled outside the Philadelphia State House into national debates for and against a federal government. These arguments were published in newspapers and pamphlets across America, giving farmers, merchants, and all future Americans the tools to debate their worth. The Federalists and Anti-Federalists took to the national stage to discuss their views.[31] In the very first sentence of the *Federalist Papers*,[32] a collection of essays and arguments in favor of the United States Constitution, Alexander Hamilton invited Americans to embrace this different way of deciding: "You are called upon to deliberate on a new Constitution ... "[33] Ordinary citizens and future Presidents weighed in on both sides.

And yet the Constitution was only the initial deliberative act. To become the law of the land, the Founders built within the ratification process further mechanisms for deliberation in the states. There could be no federal Constitution without the agreement of the various states. Thus state ratifying conventions were envisioned within the formal Constitution:

> *The ratification of the conventions of nine states, shall be*
> *sufficient for the establishment of this constitution between*
> *the states so ratifying the same. (Article VII)*

In each state, local bodies were elected with the sole responsibility to deliberate on the merits of the Constitution. Delaware became "the First State," ratifying the Constitution on December 7, 1787.[34] The requirement of further forums for discussion all across the country meant that ordinary citizens had to decide on the legitimacy of the proposed federal government. State delegates to these new state ratifying conventions were elected for the purpose of continued collective deliberation. To create our country we had to deliberate about deliberation. To sustain our country, the Constitution designed places to practice this method of decision making.

Deliberative Practice: Civic Practice

The easiest place to see these practice areas is in the Constitution's emphasis on juries. As should now be clear, juries are the central means by which "we the people" deliberate over how the law should be applied. Article III, Section 2, provides that "[t]he trial of all crimes . . . shall be by jury." The Fifth Amendment requires an indictment from a "Grand Jury." The Sixth Amendment establishes that "[i]n all criminal prosecutions, the accused shall enjoy the right to a speedy and public trial by an impartial jury." The Seventh Amendment provides in civil suits, "the right of a trial by jury shall be preserved." It is the process of jury deliberation that teaches us how to think like a citizen.

In parallel fashion, the Constitution protected institutions of citizen deliberation. Local town meetings were preserved to allow democratic decision making. Community associations were recognized as places to practice assembly and debate. Grand juries, churches, even state militia bodies were protected to allow spaces for local bodies to collectively decide important issues. Like local juries, the Framers designed spaces to practice deliberation.

The Deliberative Body

As John Adams stated, "representative government and trial by jury are the heart and lungs of liberty."[35] It only makes sense that a country formed out of deliberation would create a government based on deliberation. Deliberation is front and center in the creation of the "legislative powers" mentioned in Article I, Section 1, of the Constitution. What is Congress but a center of national deliberation? At its core, Congress exists as a forum for debate about national issues. That means every two years your vote reaffirms the issues you want addressed in hours upon hours of formal debate. Issues become law only after lots of talk on C-SPAN. While we may complain that Congress talks too much and does too little, that is part of the constitutional structure. Appropriately enough, in Article I, Section 2, the leader of the House of Representatives is called the "Speaker." The Senate is known as "the deliberative body"[36] because of the lengthy procedural mechanisms required to pass laws, and because Senate rules allow for unlimited speech by any Senator.[37] The deliberation is built within the structure of having a bicameral system of government. Congress is a purposely slow institution so that the proposed laws are carefully considered.

And despite popular cynicism, it is within the Senate and House chambers that our symbol of political deliberation remains most pure. Internal congressional deliberations are explicitly protected by Article 1, Section 6, which immunizes Senators and Representatives for what they say in political debate:

> *They shall in all cases, except treason, felony and breach of the peace, be privileged from arrest during their attendance at the session of their respective houses, and in going to and returning from the same; and for any speech or debate in either house, they shall not be questioned in any other place.*

The Speech and Debate Clause originally was created to protect legislators from charges of sedition or libel that had arisen in British parliamentary sessions.[38] Protection from civil or criminal lawsuits ensured that all legislative ideas could be discussed without fear of reprisal. It also reaffirmed the goal of sustained and open debate about proposed laws before enactment. Throughout the years, the Speech and Debate Clause has guaranteed that dissenting voices are part of the national debate, no matter how critical or disruptive to the majority government.

Congressional Juries: Impeachment

Sometimes the principle of legislative deliberation intersects with the responsibilities of juries in moments of national significance—as in the impeachment of our national leader. Right in the Constitution there is the mechanism for the impeachment of the President by a "congressional jury." And it is a deliberative process. The Constitution sets out the requirement that the Senate acts as a jury for the President:

> *The President, Vice President and all civil officers of the United States, shall be removed from office on impeachment for, and conviction of, treason, bribery, or other high crimes and misdemeanors. (Article II, Section 4)*

> *The Senate shall have the sole power to try all impeachments ... When the President of the United States is tried, the Chief Justice shall preside: And no person shall be convicted without the concurrence of two thirds of the members present. (Article I, Section 3)*

In our most serious crises, we revert to the constitutional principle of jury deliberation for a national deliberative moment. In 1868 President Andrew Johnson escaped impeachment by one vote.[39] In 1998 President Bill Clinton avoided impeachment by a more significant margin.[40] In both cases, the Senate deliberated as a public jury to determine the fitness of a President.

Deliberative Change: Amendments

Drafting the Constitution was a deliberative act that envisioned future deliberative events. The Founders knew change to be necessary and built within the constitutional structure a process of amendment. Our first ten Amendments enshrined as the Bill of Rights exist as but the most prominent of our constitutional Amendments. In over two hundred years, we have had twenty-seven such deliberative moments.[41]

Article V of the Constitution provides that by a two-thirds vote of the House and Senate, or on application by the legislatures of two-thirds of the states, a constitutional change can be proposed:

> *The Congress, whenever, two thirds of both houses shall deem it necessary, shall propose Amendments to this Constitution, or on the application of the legislatures of two thirds of the several states, shall call a convention for proposing Amendments.*

A constitutional amendment is then voted on by the conventions called for the purpose. If three-fourths of the states agree to this deliberative change, it becomes binding. The method of constitutional change is, in essence, a sustained discussion throughout the states in local conventions. We all get to think together as citizens to determine if we want to reshape our most fundamental laws.

Why Deliberation Matters
Better Judgments

Does the deliberative process create better decisions? From over fifty years of studying jury deliberations, the answer (fortunately) appears to be yes.[42] Numerous studies have examined the reasoning and results from all sorts of jury sources, with the conclusion that deliberation creates a better and more accurate result.[43] The question is, why are twelve heads better than one?[44]

One answer is that each juror can bring different judgments from the community to bear on the facts at issue: "The deliberation provides an excellent opportunity for jury members to influence one another on the meaning of facts and the value judgments implicit within them."[45] Similarly, studies have concluded that group deliberation results in a better recall of evidence than that of a single fact finder.[46] Each person is able to bring to the table a separate memory of the facts. The collected facts add up to a more complete picture of the trial testimony. In addition, with the greater number of people, personal biases tend to be minimized. As the Supreme Court recognized:

> Generally, a positive correlation exists between group size and the quality of both group performance, and group productivity. . . . When individual and group decision-making were compared, it was seen that groups performed better because prejudices of individuals were frequently counterbalanced, and objectivity resulted.[47]

Essentially, the deliberative review of evidence creates a kind of "check and balance" process, whereby the intuitions of each juror are checked and rechecked against those of the others. Only when there is consensus on the evidence can the jury deliver its verdict.

Studies have shown that especially in jurisdictions that require unanimous jury verdicts, the process of deliberation creates a more thoughtful and open search for a consensus decision.[48] In addition, it appears that minority voices participate more, and the entire jury shares an acceptance of the final result.[49]

Your deliberation as a jury thus results not only in a better decision, but also in everyone feeling better about the decision. Deliberation to unanimity makes it easier to decide because the group shares the burden of decision.[50] In addition, it is easier for jurors to return to their community having the support of their fellow jurors, who all voted the same way.[51] And no matter the decision, a jury's deliberation is good practice for the other deliberative tasks set out in the constitutional structure. If you can reach agreement through jury deliberation, you have a model for the more complex decisions of a democracy.

Jury Moments

Having spoken with many mostly happy jurors who were proud of their decision making (and only a few frustrated jurors that had some difficulty), the following common-sense advice seems to be a fair distillation of their experience. *Tip 1*: Happy jurors approach the discussion open to the challenge of different ideas. Jurors often observe the exact same witness and take away markedly different meanings from the testimony.[52] The resulting discussion is to be encouraged as an honest disagreement based on equally legitimate perceptions. *Tip 2*: Happy jurors recognize that the final decision will build on their ideas, but will not be their idea. The collaborative nature of the process almost always shapes the end result. *Tip 3*: Happy jurors recognize that the differences in approach, life experience, and values are precisely why we have juries. It is not supposed to be a rubber stamp or rejection of the case presented by the lawyers. Any difficulty in the discussion represents the strength of the system, not a weakness. *Tip 4*: Happy jurors recognize that civility is the most valuable of values that a juror can bring to the table. Jurors should recognize that each juror has an equal right to contribute, and that they must remain respectful of any differences. *Tip 5*: Happy jurors engage the debate. The process of deliberation means a sustained, interpersonal discussion that at the end produces a final decision. Each part—the debate, discussion, and decision—is important.

Even if you believe that deliberation improves decision making, it still may be difficult to see how it will work in practice. Why would a group of strangers be able to come together and resolve a contested and difficult problem? What is it about jury deliberations that allows for an increased ability to solve problems? Why would you be successful at deliberating in a jury when you are regularly unable to agree on a family vacation or business strategy?

One reason for the success of jury decisions is that during these "jury moments" jurors retain a heightened sense of focus, commitment, and responsibility. You have, after all, been given more power than you would usually be given in your regular life. You have been given judicial power. Deciding the liberty of another person, weighing the appropriate level of damages, or resolving contested facts is not something we do every day.

Jurors must rise to the occasion. Many a juror has confided that during the hours of deliberation, they thought harder than they ever had to think in their lives.[53] There is no television, Internet, or other distractions. Literally, you are required to remain focused on one issue for days upon days of sustained discussion. Rarely in life are you locked into a room and required to answer a question before you get out. There is no escape. There is no release. And it is terribly important.

This responsibility to deliberate also requires humility. By definition, you begin without a final answer. It is the process of deliberation that creates a solution. Like the creative process of a democracy, deliberation necessitates a continued discussion and always the possibility of change. It informs a process of thinking and seeing the world. If you start seeing collaborative opportunities for decisions, you will see that those decisions aren't permanent and can be amended. The process is what matters.

It is how we improve as thinkers and as citizens. Again, like the fluid nature of a democratic state, there is no right answer, but just the best-reasoned insight of the people over time.

In his final address to the Constitutional Convention, Benjamin Franklin recognized the limits of deliberation (and the Constitution). Addressing the assembled Founders, he questioned, "For when you assemble a number of men to have the advantage of their joint wisdom, you inevitably assemble with those men, all their prejudices, their passions, their errors of opinion, their local interests, and their selfish views. From such an assembly, can a perfect production be expected?"[54] The answer was of course no, but with the understanding that even with its imperfections,[55] deliberation among differences was the best method for decision making. It turned out to be the best method to create a Constitution. It was the most effective way to decide among competing visions about the most fundamental issues of the day. It still is. And if we get it wrong, we can just lock ourselves in a room and deliberate about a better solution.

*It is the ferment of ideas, the clash of disagreeing
judgments, the privilege of the individual to develop his
own thought and shape his own character which makes
progress possible.*

—Calvin Coolidge

United States Post Office and Custom House (1940) Completed in 1913
SUPERVISING ARCHITECT: James Knox Taylor
Still in use by the United States Bankruptcy Court for the Southern
District of California. Renamed the Jacob Weinberger United States
Courthouse in 1986.

SOURCE: NATIONAL ARCHIVES, RG 121-BS, BOX 9, FOLDER R, PRINT 2

7

Protecting a Dissenting Voice

A Single Voice

In the Academy Award–nominated movie *12 Angry Men*, a single juror convinces the other eleven to question their assumptions of guilt in what appears to be a simple case.[1] The lone juror dissents to prolong a quick vote for guilt, and eventually creates enough questions to turn around the verdict. When questioned about his initial "not guilty" vote, Henry Fonda, playing the juror, states, "There were eleven votes for guilty. It's not easy for me to raise my hand and send a boy off to die without talking about it first . . . [W]e're talking about somebody's life here. I mean, we can't decide in five minutes. Supposing we're wrong."[2] The movie remains canonical in the American perception of the jury.[3] It provides one of the few thoughtful, if fictionalized, versions of jury deliberations ever filmed.[4] It also connects to the very American ideal of the dissenting voice.

It might seem odd to talk about dissenting voices after an entire chapter on the importance of consensus-powered deliberations. Yet the tension between deliberation and dissent has always been part of the constitutional system. Respect for individual expression, both as a means to protect the autonomy of an individual, and as a mechanism to change the minds of others, is central to our system of democratic self-government. Similarly, an encouragement to hold unpopular or unconventional beliefs is central to the protections of the First Amendment's Freedom of Conscience Clauses.

If you study the jury instructions, you will see this interplay between group consensus and individual conscience. Examine, for example, the instruction on "unanimity" given at the end of most criminal cases.[5] Initially, the court will instruct all jurors in a criminal case that the verdict must be unanimous. The wording differs from court to court, but the core understanding is that all twelve members of the jury must agree—guilty or not guilty. Historically, all criminal juries required unanimous decisions.[6] The tradition dates all the way back to the fourteenth century,[7] and for most of our legal history state and federal courts required unanimity for criminal conviction.[8] This changed in 1972, when the Supreme Court allowed states to experiment with less than unanimous verdicts.[9] Currently, all federal courts and forty-eight of the fifty states require unanimous verdicts for felony cases (Louisiana and Oregon are the two outliers).[10]

If, however, during deliberations a jury has difficulty reaching a verdict, the tension between the group and the individual becomes heightened. In such a situation when a jury cannot reach a unanimous verdict and signals as much to a judge, an instruction similar to the following is read:

The verdict must represent the considered judgment of each juror. Your verdict, whether it be guilty or not guilty, must be unanimous.

You should make every reasonable effort to reach a verdict. In doing so, you should consult with one another, express your own views, and listen to the opinions of your fellow jurors. Discuss your differences with an open mind. Do not hesitate to re-examine your own views and change your opinion if you come to believe it is wrong.

But you should not surrender your honest beliefs about the weight or effect of evidence solely because of the opinions of your fellow jurors or for the purpose of returning a unanimous verdict.

The twelve of you should give fair and equal consideration to all the evidence and deliberate with the goal of reaching an agreement which is consistent with the individual judgment of each juror. You are impartial judges of the facts. Your sole interest is to determine whether the government has proved its case beyond a reasonable doubt.[11]

As is plain, while unanimity is the goal of deliberations, jurors are not expected to surrender their individual beliefs about the evidence for the sake of unanimity. The goal is a final unanimous verdict, but not at the expense of individual conscience. Eventually, if the jury cannot reach a unanimous verdict, the judge will declare a mistrial and send the jury home.

The principle of freedom of conscience grows from a protected space in our constitutional system where the friction between national consensus and individual dissent can work itself out. It helped nurture unique American personalities—the transformative figures like Frederick Douglass, Harriet Beecher Stowe, Susan B. Anthony,

Rachel Carson, Martin Luther King Jr., Thurgood Marshall—people who took a dissenting voice and turned it into a majority vision (changing constitutional law along the way). This principle of freedom of conscience also has a direct connection with the early history of juries.

Juries and Freedom of Conscience

"I have done according to my conscience."[12] So ended one of the most famous jury trials on record, and began one of the most principled protests in English history. Edward Bushel directed these words to the lord mayor presiding over the trial of William Penn, a Quaker preacher and eventual founder of the state of Pennsylvania.[13] In 1670, William Penn had sought to conduct a peaceful worship at a local London church. Finding the church closed and his way blocked by soldiers, Penn decided to hold the religious service outside in the street next to the church. King Charles II ordered the service stopped.[14] Penn was arrested for violating the Conventicle Act, which banned non-sanctioned religions. He was charged with unlawful assembly and put on trial before the London Court of Session[15] for "preaching to the people and drawing a tumultuous company after them."[16]

Edward Bushel and eleven other jurors were selected to hear the case.[17] For the government, three men testified that they saw Penn and his companion William Mead on Gracechurch Street, but because of the crowd noise could not hear what they were saying.[18] While neither Penn nor Mead hid their intended religious purpose in being out on the street, both defendants chose to challenge the legality of the indictment and the fairness of the proceedings.[19] The evidence was presented and the jury was sent out to deliberate.

After about an hour and a half of deliberations, the bailiff was sent to inform the jury that the judge and lord mayor were growing impatient for the verdict.[20] A short while later the jury was summoned back into court. Asked if it had reached a verdict yet, the jury responded no. The judge then sent them back to deliberate, telling them that if they did not return with a unanimous guilty verdict that the entire jury would be locked up until morning without "meat, drink, or fire."[21] The jury retired again and debated until once again the bailiff banged on the door. The judge was asking for a verdict. The jury was again brought out into open court. When asked if they have a verdict on the unlawful assembly charge, the jury responded only, "Guilty of speaking on Gracechurch Street."[22] The court officials expressed disbelief. What about the charged offense—unlawful assembly—the court demanded? The jury's response was the same. The jury was sent back. And again after a little while they were summoned back before the court. The jury refused to change its answer for William Penn, but this time they found William Mead not guilty.[23] Furious, the judge declared, "You shall not be dismissed till we have a verdict that the court will accept; and you shall be locked up, without meat, drink, fire, or tobacco; you shall not . . . abuse the court, we will have a verdict by the help of God or you shall starve for it."[24] The jury was kept overnight. True to his threat, the judge denied all food, fire, and water. But despite the treatment, early the next morning the verdict against William Penn remained unchanged—"Guilty of speaking on Gracechurch Street."[25] Nothing more. Twice more the jury was sent out. Twice more they came back with the same verdict. Then, faced with increasing verbal abuse by the court (Edward Bushel himself was threatened with branding, indictment, and having his "nose cut off"),[26] the jury came back and found both William Penn and William Mead not guilty. Penn, Mead, and the principle of religious freedom were all vindicated.

The immediate situation for Edward Bushel and the other jurors, however, did not improve. Faced with furious court officials, they were each fined and ordered to Newgate Prison.[27] Bushel refused to pay the fine to get out of prison. For nine weeks he remained locked up under horrible conditions. His predicament was difficult but not unusual. In earlier times, if the judge disagreed with the jury's verdict the entire jury could be punished. A "writ of attaint" could issue and a new jury could be sworn in to see if the first jury got the verdict right or had committed perjury.[28]

Bushel and three other like-minded jurors thought it wrong to so punish a jury and obtained the services of a lawyer to challenge their detention. They appealed to England's Court of Common Pleas, and in a landmark decision, Chief Justice John Vaughn held that jurors may base their verdict on their own understanding of the facts and cannot be coerced into a verdict by the judge.[29] It is a decision that stands to this day—that jurors, and not the judge, render the verdict according to their consciences.

Bushel's Case mattered not only for Bushel and his fellow jurors, but also for the creation of the jury system in America. Juries became intertwined with the protection of freedom of conscience and freedom of expression.[30] In simple terms, a jury's defense of faith led to a faith in juries.

In America, the institution of the jury remained a reminder of religious freedom, even though in recent history it has been judges, and not juries, that have protected religious practices considered outside the mainstream.[31] As a parallel local power source to challenge the government,[32] juries, like the First Amendment's right to individual conscience, are facilitators of self-expression. As a space for controlled dissent, juries offer a structural mechanism to articulate and tolerate difference. As symbols of community conscience, juries are democratic counterweights to centralized power. So where does this principle of freedom of conscience come from in American thought?

Freedom of Conscience and the Constitution
Free Exercise of Faith

From its earliest days, America opened its doors to freedom of conscience. The American colonies were a haven from religious persecution in Europe. Puritans, Presbyterians, Baptists, Quakers, and Catholics all sought refuge in the New World.[33] Different and diverse religious sects and independent thinkers established new belief systems away from governmental interference. Pennsylvania established itself as a "holy experiment,"[34] becoming a Quaker colony. Catholics settled Maryland. The colonies promised religious and intellectual freedom. Yet, as these new religious groups grew in power, the tensions between faiths grew as well. In New England, Puritans hanged Quakers, banned Baptists, and burned the books of dissenting faiths.[35] Rhode Island was created by the exile of Roger Williams from the Massachusetts Bay Colony.[36] Early American history is replete with ironic examples of newly escaped religious leaders replicating the Old World intolerance in the New World.

It was with this understanding of religious strife that America developed its strikingly successful approach to freedom of conscience. First, in terms of religion, the experience of religious conflict informed the drafting of the Constitution. Article VI of the Constitution proclaims that unlike European tradition, religion must be neither a qualification nor a barrier to public office:

> *No religious test shall ever be required as a qualification to any office or public trust under the United States.*

In banning religious tests for high office, the Constitution broke from history, signaling that tolerance and free exercise of religion were separate from government and police power. In addition to Article VI, the First Amendment clearly states our aspirations of religious liberty:

> *Congress shall make no law respecting an establishment of religion, or prohibiting free exercise thereof.*

First among our great freedoms is to pray or not pray in our own way. As James Madison stated, "The Religion of every man must be left to the conviction and conscience of every man."[37] Or as the Supreme Court stated more recently, we are left to think, pray, and act as we choose: "Freedom of conscience and freedom to adhere to such religious organization or form of worship as the individual may choose cannot be restricted by law."[38]

Similarly, the government may not impose or establish a national religion. The Establishment Clause means that the government must remain neutral in matters of religious belief.[39] We may be a "faith-based" nation, but our faith comes from within rather than from the government.[40] The Constitution is the gatekeeper of personal faith, keeping direct governmental interference away from places of worship, prayers, and religious thought.

The United States stands apart because of our extreme religious tolerance. While our history is rife with personal religious tension and prejudice, it also remained relatively free from government-sponsored religious discrimination. As a constitutional matter, the Supreme Court has stated that the First Amendment means that "[n]either a state nor the federal government can set up a church. Neither can pass laws which aid one religion, aid all religions, or prefer one religion over another. Neither can force nor influence a person to go to or remain away from church against his will or force him to profess a belief or disbelief in any religion. No person can be punished for entertaining or professing religious beliefs or disbeliefs, for church attendance or non-attendance."[41] The result is that all faiths and nonbelievers are protected. Religious liberty is but an example of the deeper value of tolerance that marks us. If we can agree to disagree about our most fundamental beliefs, we can be open to disagreements about other values, lifestyles, and political ideas.[42]

One of the reasons why the First Amendment used the term "free exercise" is that James Madison did not think that "tolerance" was a strong enough protection.[43] Madison wanted more than tolerance. In essence, he wanted a country that allowed heresy—a true freedom to dissent. It was Madison who suggested that the language in the Virginia Declaration of Rights be changed from "all men should enjoy the *fullest toleration* in the exercise of religion" to "all men are equally entitled to the *free exercise* of religion."[44] As Jon Meacham explains in his book *American Gospel,* "The idea of 'toleration' bothered Madison. Liberty was the issue, not tolerance, for 'tolerance' could mean the action of allowing something or granting permission."[45]

Free Expression and Juries

In a country predicated on self-government, free expression ensures political freedom. The First Amendment sets forth the protection of speech, press, assembly, and petitioning the government for redress:

> *Congress shall make no law ... abridging the freedom of speech, or of the press, or the right of the people peaceably to assemble, and to petition the government for a redress of grievances. (First Amendment)*

As an aspiration, the First Amendment protects each of us from government control of thought, speech, and writing. As a practical ideal, it places the responsibility of political liberty in our hands. The result is that it fosters different, diverse, and dissenting voices in an ongoing debate—just like a jury.

In the Founding era, juries were the protectors of free expression. American juries stood against a British government intent on controlling critical speech through the Alien and Sedition Acts and Libel Act of the early colonies.[46] Since a libel case had to be prosecuted through a local jury, it was the jury that could essentially decide whether the criticism of the government was appropriate. As one scholar put it:

> [U]p to and even past the adoption of the first amendment, the jury was seen as the primary protector of free speech. [T]he jury's increased role in libel cases was seen as among the central principles of freedom of speech and freedom of the press. Free speech existed largely in the extent to which the people—through their surrogate, the jury—could decide how much the individual could criticize the government.[47]

This role of juries in free expression cases has shifted somewhat. Today, while juries play a limited role in determining "obscenity," and are entrusted to decide if the unwanted disclosure of private information is actionable—under a community standards test[48]—it is judges who have become the primary protectors of the First Amendment.[49]

Today, while juries are not central to First Amendment trials, there still exists an influential overlap between the role of free expression in a democracy, and the role of a jury in a democracy. First, one of the great justifications for a robust protection of free speech is that free expression fosters a search for the best ideas. Differing views compete in the marketplace of ideas and the superior ones win out.[50] Similarly, in a jury room, dissenting voices are allowed to try to convince others about the validity and strength of those ideas. Like in a democracy, each vote matters, so the most compelling and insightful arguments can have significant sway (even in the smaller marketplace of twelve votes).

A second theory of the First Amendment is that free expression fosters democracy by creating citizens educated enough for self-government. As scholars have recognized, the First Amendment allows each citizen to take part in the public debate.[51] In so doing, the First Amendment, like a jury, reinforces the principles of self-government.

A third justification for the First Amendment is that free expression can provide a means to check overreaching or abusive government. In *New York Times v. Sullivan*, Justice William Brennan asserted that Americans share "a profound national commitment to the principle that debate on public issues should be uninhibited, robust, and wide-open, and that it may well include vehement, caustic, and sometimes unpleasantly sharp attacks on government and public officials."[52] As we will see in the next chapter, the jury, albeit in a different context, plays a similar structural role in checking government power.

A fourth, related justification for the protection of free expression is that it offers a safety valve for dissent. Both the government and the public are safer if disagreements can be aired in the open, and resolved with peaceful and civil debate. As Justice Louis Brandeis stated in *Whitney v. California*:

> Those who won our independence . . . [knew] that it is hazardous to discourage thought, hope and imagination; that fear breeds repression; that repression breeds hate; that hate menaces stable government; that the path of safety lies in the opportunity to discuss

freely supposed grievances and proposed remedies; and that the fitting remedy for evil counsels is good ones.[53]

Public jury trials and the larger public legal system are a way to channel sometimes ugly conflict into civil resolution.

Finally, it must be remembered that the First Amendment does not guarantee unbounded, unstructured expression. The government is allowed to regulate hate speech, fighting words, libel, obscenity, commercial speech, speech in public and semipublic forums, television indecency, symbolic conduct, campaign speech, broadcast speech, public employee speech, viewpoint discrimination, as well as the time, place, and manner of political speech.[54] You can march down Main Street, but not at 3:00 a.m., with a marching band yelling "fire!" and holding burning pitchforks. The point is that our courts have set up a purposeful give and take between dissenting voices and the mainstream political culture. As Geoffrey Stone writes, "By allowing for ambiguity and conflict in the public sphere, the First Amendment promotes the emergence of character traits that are essential to a well-functioning democracy, including tolerance, skepticism, personal responsibility, curiosity, distrust of authority, and independence of mind."[55] The same can be said for serving on a jury.

The recognition of dissent connects two themes in our constitutional system. First, that the United States is founded on a spirit of individualism, and even in a collaborative pursuit like a democracy or a jury, differing individual views are to be nurtured. Second, while a system of decision making must make room for dissenting voices, it cannot be stymied by them. Differing viewpoints may influence a political issue in the marketplace of ideas, but to change policy those voices must convince the majority of voters. A space for dissent does not mean that the minority view controls the final decision. Similarly, dissenting voices in a jury might prevent a unanimous verdict, but the result is simply a retrial. If you do not agree, the jury hangs, and the case begins again. The legal process (like the political process) still goes forward toward a final resolution.

Why Freedom of Conscience Matters
The Cause Case

Civil lawsuits allow individuals to challenge perceived infringements of their rights. Individuals can sue governments to challenge the rights, remedies, and wrongs done to them concerning their ability to speak, curse, pray, or do any of a number of expressive activities. Burning a book, protesting a funeral, refusing to conform to some rule or regulation, all are fodder for legal challenge. In First Amendment cases involving religion or free speech, the most disempowered minority can be given voice to challenge the greatest power sources in the country.[56] And we listen. We empanel juries to hear this individual calling out into the legal wilderness. We ask citizens to judge the claims of others—even when it is clear that the voice is not the community voice, and may in fact be challenging the dominant community belief system. We do so not always because we think the speaker is correct, but because we believe in the value of allowing the person to protest.

On a few occasions, I have represented individuals who have chosen to protest (or express their views) through the criminal justice system. Usually these cases involve free speech claims of protesting without a permit and are treated as unlawful assembly charges in court. Usually there is a targeted event to protest and a less targeted plan for civil disobedience.

As defense cases go, they tend to be losing efforts as the law is against the clients, and the purpose is to protest rather than to mount a meritorious legal defense. Most protesters know they might be arrested. Yet many are surprised to be prosecuted in criminal court for the offense. As a legal system, we don't distinguish between politically motivated offenses and regular criminal offenses. The result is that many times a group of protesters ends up in the mix of a regular criminal courtroom. There is nothing like walking into Monday morning lockup and seeing a line of disoriented protestors behind a row of despondent prostitutes.

Counseling these clients offers its own challenges, as most of the time the defendants want to justify their actions to the jury or judge—and such explanations are not always limited to the legally relevant facts. While one may have protested against a war, the prosecution or defense has nothing to do with the rightness or wrongness of the war, or the righteousness of the protest. The law cares about whether you protested unlawfully. Thus lawyers must recalibrate their strategy to recognize that protesters care most about being heard. They want someone—a jury or a judge—to understand why they did what they did, regardless of whether there was a legal basis. Sometimes this can engender sympathy from the jurors, but usually winning or losing is beside the point.

What is most striking is that at the end of these cases, clients (even those who lose) tend to be more satisfied with the legal process than even some clients who win in normal criminal contexts. The fact that the court gave them a forum to be heard, to express their views, and to challenge the system creates a sense of respect that quiets the outrage. Dissenting within the system provides them the result they wanted. In one case I tried, a judge actually apologized to the protestors for being compelled by law to convict them and wished them well in their continued principled stand for conscience. The protestors—newly minted convicted "criminals"—stood there with smiles of contentment as they listened to the judge pronounce her guilty verdict. It was an amazing moment as the internal tension between dissent and the rule of law played out before me.

Perhaps my favorite jury trial of all time involved the unlikely prosecution of a wheelchair-bound homeless man who had been arrested for singing in a train station (and then demanding payment for his performance). The transit police had asked him to stop and when he refused, they wheeled him out of the station. In protest, he wheeled himself back in and was arrested for the crime of unlawful entry. Thus began one of the least significant and most meaningful jury trials of my career. Why this misdemeanor trial, in a city with a significant crime problem, made it to a jury is another question, but it did. The alleged crime was straightforward. He was asked to leave. He did not leave. He was arrested. The defense also was straightforward. He had a right to free expression. Singing was expression. Police could not arbitrarily remove someone for expression. The jury was asked to resolve this tension between social order and free expression.

As good lawyers, both the prosecutor and I focused our efforts on intricate arguments about First Amendment principles, municipal regulations, and the placement of placards regulating disruptive behaviors in the train station. Was singing speech? Couldn't it be regulated? What were the rules for impromptu personal expressions? For three days, the legal energies and financial resources of the court system turned on this rather trivial event. But for my client it was about one thing: explaining to folks who usually walked right past him why he was a person deserving of attention and respect. For my client, what mattered was the forum for his humanity. He testified. He smiled (a rare event for a man with a difficult life). And he almost sang. In the end, after three long days of deliberation the jury could not make a decision. They were evenly divided between our opposing theories. A mistrial was declared. As we walked out of the courthouse, there was but one sound, a happy tune being sung by my client as he headed back toward the train station.

A Matter of Self-Respect

After the evidence is presented, with the pressure of an expected verdict, the jury room seems to have less free space for dissenting opinions. A lot of time and effort gets put into reaching a jury decision. The incentive for dissenting jurors to change their minds is great. Research has shown that the 12 Angry Men situation of having a single juror convince the others is less common than the reverse, where the majority of jurors sway the dissenting juror.[57] In fact, it appears that in cases that start off 11–1 for one outcome, it rarely happens that the jury switches all the way back to the other view.[58] Part of this phenomenon involves the pressure put on by fellow jurors, and part is the reasonable desire for a unanimous opinion. The emphasis put on a final verdict is real, and the system certainly finds it more efficient if the first jury to hear the case makes the decision. While judges will no longer lock juries up without "meat, drink, or fire," sometimes the pressure on the "holdout" juror is intense.

I once talked to a juror in a civil case who had held out for two full days against the others in the jury room. An experienced litigator, an exceptionally reasonable and charming guy, he said it took every ounce of strength not to cave to the increasing pressure of the other jurors. Each hour passed so slowly, each argument about the law had been parsed so carefully, that the jurors eventually resorted to reading the newspaper to avoid destroying the last bits of civility left when the judge sent them back for even more deliberations. This experience is actually rather atypical, as research has shown that juries rarely deadlock because of one or two holdouts, but rather because there is a greater split among the group.[59]

The result of a holdout juror can of course lead to a less than constructive result. It can, in fact, turn ugly. As one holdout in a high-profile criminal trial described, it was "positively poison": "They shouted at me. One of the jurors threatened me. He turned on me in a fury, just a fury, and he said, 'I'm going to spend the rest of my life destroying you.'"[60] Such passion is extreme, but a by-product of the serious investment of energy that many jurors expend in deliberations. There are times, of course, when a juror simply refuses to deliberate. The issue is not a disagreement over the evidence, an interpretation of the law, or weakness in the case, but some other moral or mental problem. Occasionally, a juror will slip through voir dire who has a hidden (or at least unspoken) antagonism toward the judicial system or one of the parties. Jurors who refuse to deliberate or who obstinately refuse to consider the views of others do not create a pleasant deliberative experience. There is not much that can be done about it, as judges are quite reluctant to remove jurors during deliberations. Usually, it results in a frustrating time for the jury and a retrial for the parties.

On the other hand, sometimes a holdout juror's stand results in a more just outcome. The Honorable William L. Dwyer, a federal judge and author of *In the Hands of the People: The Trial Jury's Origins, Triumphs, Troubles, and Future in American Democracy*, tells a story of one such case:

> Charlie Renton, as I will call him, was a federal prisoner in California. Renton had spent years in jail for recurring episodes of unarmed bank robbery and drug dealing, all to finance his enthusiastic pursuit of liquor, drugs, and women. Now in middle age, he seemed old beyond his years, burned out,

institutionalized, and affable. But Renton was seeth-
ing over an injustice. Before his latest trip to prison
he had entrusted a drinking buddy and fellow drug
dealer with $2,500, to hold for him until he got out.
The friend, predictably, had spent the money. Renton
now wanted it back. . . . Renton mailed a letter from
prison, telling the erstwhile friend what he would do
to him (death or at least irreversible damage to his private parts) if the money was not repaid. There was no
response, so Renton mailed a second threatening letter, and then a third.

A federal prosecution followed, and it was severe
beyond any apparent need. Renton obviously had no
ability to carry out his threats, he was locked up. . . .
[H]e was charged with six federal felonies (two per
letter); three counts of threatening violence to collect
an extension of credit (in violation of a statute aimed
chiefly at mob extortion), and three of sending threats
through the mail.[61]

Judge Dwyer tells how this case played out in his Seat-
tle courtroom. In his defense Renton testified and called
himself "an old fool," and that he had been merely "blow-
ing off steam" in a frustrating and helpless situation.[62]
Under the law, Renton's intent mattered, but it did not
make a difference whether Renton had the present ability
to carry out his threat. After prolonged deliberations, the
jury could not reach a verdict. A mistrial was declared.
Curious about what appeared to be a rather simple case,
with the evidence pointing toward Renton's guilt, Judge
Dwyer invited the jury foreman to come to his chambers.[63] The foreman explained:

All twelve jurors, he said, felt that the case was too
trivial to be in court—that it had been grievously over-
charged and was an imposition on their time and the

judge's. Eleven of them, however, decided that under
the law and the evidence there was no choice but to
convict on all six counts. Only the foreman disagreed.
At first he had trouble formulating why. It was a matter of self-respect: "I had to live with myself—the one
in the mirror." Then he thought of all the vile language
he had heard for years while working on construction
projects, and on the street in his downtown neighborhood. Nearly all of it was hot air—mere expressions of
emotion. What Renton had written to his debtor, the
foreman decided, was "no more than whiskey talk or
a figure of speech—not to be taken literally." It was, in
other words, not a threat at all but merely an outburst,
"in language common to both their vocabularies." In
this way the foreman reconciled his sense of justice
with the jury instructions. And he stood his ground. It
was uncomfortable, but "my honor to myself was more
important than what the eleven thought of me."[64]

While the discomfort is real, the mechanism for having this dissenting voice is part of the system. A hung
jury "represents the legal system's respect for the minority
viewpoint that is held strongly enough to thwart the will
of the majority."[65] It also can result in a fair outcome. In
the Renton case, after the hung jury, Renton was allowed
to plead to a single count of sending a letter through the
mail, and received a small increase in his sentence. As
Judge Dwyer concluded, "The jury deadlocked by a vote
of eleven to one. But the result, in the end, was fairer than
it would have been without the foreman's dissent."[66]

Practicing Free Exercise in the Jury Room
The religious melting pot that is the United States works
because we have learned to accept the duality that faith
and liberty of conscience can coexist.[67] As Jon Meacham
recognized, Americans share a "public religion" or "civic

religion" that allows faith to be unifying and tolerant.[68] By a public religion, we mean a belief system that allows us to have things like "In God We Trust" on our money, to say "One Nation Under God" in our Pledge of Allegiance, and to allow Presidents to end each speech with "May God Bless America."[69] A public religion means acceptance of congressional chaplains, the Ten Commandments displayed in the Supreme Court, and a religiously vibrant society, all without insulting people of other faiths or nonbelievers. Purposely, we do not define which "god" we are talking about, nor do we specify which religious belief is controlling. At the same time, we allow private religious beliefs to flourish in whatever manner they see fit. Members of squarely antithetical and antagonistic faiths live side by side, free to believe that the devil is their neighbor, and yet required to tolerate the free exercise of the other's beliefs. It is a system that encourages different faiths to mix and yet remain true to their differing individual consciences.

A parallel can be made to your jury experience. All jurors (hopefully) come into their jury service with the shared belief that they will contribute to a just outcome. What "justice" means is not defined and might not be clear until you hear the particular facts, the law, and the case presented, but there is a faith in a larger sense of justice. Each juror hopes that by applying the law to the facts within a fair process, some measure of justice will be obtained. Yet at the same time, we do not require each juror to see the facts or understand the law in the exact same way. We allow for different beliefs. We even allow for squarely antithetical beliefs to sit side by side. This probably does not mean we want jurors to be the civic equivalent of a fringe religious fanatic, but, in truth, it is hard to prevent it. The hope is that in accepting the same duality of allowing different beliefs to coexist under a larger shared belief system, we can encourage that same sort of respect for other people's differing opinions.

Regardless of whether James Madison chose to use the term "tolerance" in the First Amendment, the principle of toleration remains a part of our national character. Juries are but a concentrated practice area for the skill of tolerance. To be able to avoid divisiveness without sacrificing principle is one of the most difficult and important challenges of a democracy. It is also one of the greatest challenges of jury deliberations. How the juror decides is up to his or her conscience, and the rest of the jury (and society) must understand and value it. The free exercise of differing views—including dissenting opinions—in a jury room is to be expected and encouraged.

Are twelve heads better than one? Yes, and not just because twelve jurors collectively are more perceptive than the judge. The jury brings fresh energy and a current of common sense, of elemental fairness, into the stream of justice; it brings not just group intelligence and dialogue but community values.
—William L. Dwyer

United States Post Office and Court House (1900) Completed in 1889
SUPERVISING ARCHITECTS: Mifflin E. Bell and Will. A. Freret
The United States District Court for the District of New Hampshire met here until 1967; the United States Circuit Court for the District of New Hampshire met here until that court was abolished in 1912. Now in use as the state's Legislative Office Building.

SOURCE: NATIONAL ARCHIVES, RG 121-BA, BOX 11, PRINT 948

8

Judging Accountability

A Seat of Judgment

You sit in judgment. Literally and figuratively you sit—twelve jurors judging a human being or human problem. While your seats may not be as elevated as the judge's, your position is just as important. As you sit in that jury box, across from the defendant or plaintiff, you act as judge. Sure, no one gave you a black robe, but you act as a force for accountability. You represent the community—a community conscience.[1] As jurors, your responsibility is to hold someone accountable. You bear witness to the violation of the community order. In a criminal case, the government has alleged a violation of a societal rule—a legal norm. In a civil case, one party to the lawsuit has alleged a breach of law—a negligent act, a broken promise. A juror holds the parties in both cases accountable. If you think about the premise of law—criminal or civil—it exists as a mechanism to hold people responsible for breaking the rules. A juror thus sits in judgment to decide the legal and moral blameworthiness of an individual or entity.

Judgment involves an awesome, unfamiliar power. In my criminal cases, jurors would comment that there had been no harder decision than to pass final judgment on another life.[2] It is not unusual to see tears or flushed faces at the end of a case. Jurors write letters weeks or months later still trying to process the weight of final judgment. Everyone knows the irrevocable consequences of a verdict. Similarly, some civil cases have resulted in irreversible financial damage to the losing party. In 1984, Pennzoil sued Texaco over a contract dispute. The jury awarded an $11.1 *billion* judgment against Texaco.[3] The size of the damages award (even after being reduced by an appellate court) forced Texaco into bankruptcy.[4] A handful of jurors helped end the financial life of a billion-dollar company. While the Texaco/Pennzoil result is not typical, the jury system does give ordinary citizens tremendous legal authority to hold a wrongdoer accountable.

Yet jurors also have another role. The jury holds the legal system accountable. In our system, the jury is the ultimate check on government power. The Sixth and Seventh Amendments are reservations of constitutional power to citizens. Those Amendments assert that the power to judge—to decide for the community—is reserved for the people.

In criminal cases, jurors stand between the entire prosecutorial power of the state and the individual accused of a crime. A jury determines if the government has proved its case—has met its "burden of proof" to prove guilt "beyond a reasonable doubt."[5] That means that the government has a constitutional obligation to develop sufficient evidence to convince each juror of guilt beyond a reasonable doubt. A defense lawyer need not introduce evidence, cross-examine witnesses, or give an opening statement or closing argument—the entire burden rests on the government.

The Supreme Court has held that "proof beyond a reasonable doubt" is one of the fundamental rights guaranteed by the Due Process Clause.[6] It puts the highest standard of proof between the government and the individual, and remains one of "the fundamental principles that are deemed essential for the protection of life and liberty."[7] If the jury is not convinced beyond a reasonable doubt, the jury holds the government accountable by finding the defendant not guilty. As the Supreme Court concluded in establishing the "beyond a reasonable doubt" standard as a constitutional requirement, "Use of the reasonable doubt standard is indispensable to command the respect and confidence of the community in applications of the criminal law. It is critical that the moral force of the criminal law not be diluted by a standard of proof that leaves people in doubt about whether innocent men are being condemned. It is also important in our free society that every individual going about his ordinary affairs have confidence that his government cannot adjudge him guilty of a criminal offense without convincing a proper fact-finder of his guilt with utmost certainty."[8]

It is an odd and extraordinary structural power. If you think about it, in any federal criminal case, the Executive Branch authorities have brought criminal charges against an individual. Paid professionals—prosecutors and police—use constitutional powers to arrest and charge a defendant. The laws have been created and passed by duly elected members of the Legislative Branch. These laws represent a democratic statement of law and order. A judge, representing the Judicial Branch, presides over the trial brought by the government. Yet the jury, ordinary citizens selected from the community, can decide the case against the collective wishes of the executive, legislative, and judicial powers. The jury can say that's not good enough, we need more evidence to get us beyond a reasonable doubt. You have to go through us for a conviction.[9] The jury has the power to acquit despite the wishes of all three branches of government.

The Founders designed a structural protection that gives citizens the ultimate moral and legal enforcement of the law. Just as people vote for their legislative and executive representatives, the jury keeps the judiciary in the hands of the people.[10]

Further, because the Double Jeopardy Clause prevents a retrial, once the jury acquits, the decision is unreviewable.[11] This power protects against a vengeful state that might seek to keep punishing those who caused it trouble:

> *Nor shall any person be subject for the same offense to be twice put in jeopardy of life and limb. (Fifth Amendment)*

Jury verdicts are final. The Double Jeopardy Clause means that we need not defend ourselves against repetitive prosecutions. But why did we entrust jurors with such an important and outsized power of accountability?

The Trial of John Peter Zenger

A single case in the early part of American history helped shape the ideal of the American jury.[12] In 1734 a struggling newspaper printer named John Peter Zenger became a symbol of the power and independence of American juries. Zenger published the *New York Weekly Journal*, a newspaper that began running articles and letters critical of the Royal Governor of New York, William Cosby.[13] At the time, tension was growing between the American colonies and the British government that Cosby personified. Governor Cosby had arrived in New York in 1732, and in short order began making enemies with local political interests.[14] In response, Zenger's paper devoted itself to harsh criticism of the Governor's actions, labeling him a tyrant and a crook.[15] By 1735 the Governor had had enough of the ridicule and ordered Zenger arrested for "seditious libel" (the publishing of comments deemed a threat to the government or public order).[16] He commanded that copies of the *New York Weekly Journal* be burned.[17]

Zenger's work, however, had already influenced the community, making his prosecution more difficult. In direct defiance of the Governor's wishes, two colonial grand juries refused to indict Zenger for the crime of seditious libel. The grand juries rejected the government's accusations. Undeterred, the Governor circumvented the grand jury process and had Zenger charged by "information" and prosecuted him before a local criminal jury.[18]

The criminal jury trial pitted the Attorney General, representing the Governor's interests, against Zenger and his attorney, Andrew Hamilton, a prominent Philadelphian.[19] Zenger faced an uphill battle. The law of seditious libel was squarely against Zenger's position. At the time of the trial, "truth" could not be used as a defense against seditious libel.[20] The crime was considered completed by merely publishing the offending words. Unlike modern libel law, even if the Governor was in fact a "crook" and a "tyrant," the only fact that mattered legally was the publication. Thus Andrew Hamilton had a difficult charge to convince a jury that Zenger's actions were not criminal.

This battle was made tougher because Hamilton conceded at the outset that Zenger had, in fact, published the offending materials.[21] Further, consistent with the existing law, the judge refused to allow Hamilton to put on any defense that would show the truth of the libelous statements.[22] Yet instead of conceding defeat, Hamilton spoke directly to the jury about the jury. Hamilton reminded them of famous British cases in which juries stood up for people voicing their conscience. He even referenced the Bushel jury that acquitted William Penn.[23]

Hamilton argued that to criticize the government "is a right which all freeman claim . . . [that] they have a right publicly to remonstrate the abuses of power in the strongest terms."[24] Hamilton pointed out that the institution of the jury had been established to correct for the power of government leaders. The jury had been created because good Englishmen "saw clearly the danger of trusting their liberties and properties to be tried, even by the greatest men in the kingdom without the judgment of a jury of their equals. They have felt the terrible effects of leaving it to the judgment of those great men to say what was scandalous and seditious, false or ironical."[25] Finally, Hamilton empowered the jury to see its own place within the legal system, as the voice of the community (in this case the American community as opposed to the oppressive British community):

> [This] is not the case of a poor printer, nor of New York alone, which you are now trying. No. It may in its consequence affect every freeman that lives under a British government on the main of America. It is the best cause. It is the cause of liberty and I make no doubt but your upright conduct this day will not only entitle you to the love and esteem of your fellow citizens; but every man who prefers freedom to a life of slavery will bless and honor you as men who have battled the attempt of tyranny.[26]

The jury quickly acquitted Zenger.

This influential case helped shaped the ideal of the jury in America. Some scholars suggest that the *Zenger* case alone inspired the First Amendment's protection of free speech and press, the Fifth Amendment's requirement of grand jury indictments, and the Sixth Amendment's

right to a public, local jury trial.[27] It portrayed the jury
as a heroic institution—a bulwark against tyranny. As the
Supreme Court recognized, looking at this early history
of America:

> A right to jury trial is granted to criminal defendants
> in order to prevent oppression by the Government.
> Those who wrote our constitutions knew from history
> and experience that it was necessary to protect against
> unfounded criminal charges brought to eliminate
> enemies and against judges too responsive to the voice
> of higher authority ... Providing an accused with
> the right to be tried by a jury of his peers gave him
> an inestimable safeguard against the corrupt or over-
> zealous prosecutor and against the compliant, biased
> or eccentric judge. If the defendant preferred the com-
> mon-sense judgment of a jury to the more tutored but
> perhaps less sympathetic reaction of the single judge,
> he was to have it.[28]

As a historical caveat to the *Zenger* trial, it must be
mentioned that juries in early America had the power to
decide both the facts *and the law*. In those times, before
the legal system had developed into its current formalized, professional structure, more power had been left in
the hands of the jury. Even judges at the time were not
necessarily trained lawyers—thus educated citizens had
some claim to be able to decide legal principles. From
1814 to 1818, a blacksmith, not a lawyer, sat on the highest
court of Rhode Island, and from 1819 to 1826 a farmer was
the court's Chief Justice.[29] Early practice gave more leeway for lawyers, like Andrew Hamilton, to argue that the
jury could interpret the law. While it is clear that Hamilton played to the political sympathies of the jury, there
was at the time more latitude for juries to decide legal
issues, including the definition of crimes at the time.[30]

In contrast, modern juries are required to find the facts, not to determine the law. Courts have restrained the authority (although not the power) of juries to decide the law.[31] The professionalized justice system with trained judges, standardized legal instructions, and a more defined role for juries, means that juries today are expected to apply the law set forth by the judge. Nevertheless, while the authority to decide the law has been taken away, the power of the jury to issue the final verdict has not. The jury still holds the system accountable. But where does this principle of accountability come from in our constitutional system?

Accountability and Constitutional Structure

At its core, the legal system is about accountability. Similarly, the Constitution establishes a structure to hold the government accountable to the people. Your vote both empowers and checks the actions of your elected leaders. But the Constitution's structural protection runs deeper than simply voting. To design an "accountable" government the Founders recognized that it was necessary to have several competing power sources. The resulting division of power and checks and balances within the constitutional system exists to create accountability and promote responsibility.

Federalism

The idea of sharing power between federal and local interests is called "federalism." As a governing theory, it offers twofold protection. First, by limiting federal authority, it prevents the concentration of centralized power. Second, by preserving state constitutions and local control over health, education, and police powers, it maximizes state power. As Justice Anthony Kennedy wrote, "Federalism was our Nation's own discovery. The Framers split the atom of sovereignty. It was the genius of their idea that our citizens would have two political capacities, one state and one federal, each protected from incursion by the other. The resulting Constitution created a legal system unprecedented in form and design."[32]

To protect against overly centralized power, the Tenth Amendment reserves all undelegated power to the states or to the people:

> *The powers not delegated to the United States by the Constitution, nor prohibited by it to the states, are reserved to the states, or to the people.*

This balance of federal and state rights presumes a constant tug of war for power. In a democracy that values active participation in government, the split between federal and state government creates two mechanisms for accountability. If we had only a large federal government, our ability to participate directly in any meaningful way would be sharply curtailed. However, through the state or local political process we have the ability to participate in the government that has the closest connection to our lives. Your Senator will not be bothered that your street lamp has gone out yet your local Alderman may care. When you feel like your local representative is not representing your interests—maybe because you are in the minority or because your views are unpopular in your community—then you still have the option of petitioning the federal government for change. This kind of dual accountability increases the chances that your voice will be heard.

Federalism also recognizes that the answers to society's problems may not be the same everywhere. Federalism allows not only for direct accountability and connection, but also the space to create, experiment, and develop differing answers to social problems. Fundamental issues are decided state by state (in legislatures and juries). Different states have taken different approaches to taxes, marriage, health insurance, and public schools. At the same time, we have federal laws that also control those politically charged areas. This split between federal and state power enhances the connection of individual citizens, and encourages creativity and diversity in state governance. It also creates more efficient and responsive government leaders who compete to be accountable to the citizens that elect them. In parallel, our state and federal jury system ensures local control within a national justice system.

Separation of Powers

Federalism is but one of the checks against concentrated government authority. The Constitution is a document built on a carefully crafted separation of powers. Article I creates the Legislative Branch (which writes the laws). Article II creates the Executive Branch (which executes the laws). Article III creates the Judicial Branch (which interprets the laws and resolves the conflicts among the branches):

> *All legislative powers herein granted shall be vested in a Congress of the United States, which shall consist of a Senate and House of Representatives. (Article I, Section 1)*

> *The executive power shall be vested in a President of the United States of America. (Article II, Section 1)*

> *The judicial power of the United States shall be vested in one Supreme Court, and in such inferior courts as the Congress may from time to time ordain and establish. (Article III, Section 1)*

Among the branches there are numerous internal checks on power.[33] For example, Article I delineates the specific powers of Congress. For a law to go into effect, both the Senate and House of Representatives must pass it (Article I, Section 7). Our bicameral legislative system provides its own internal check. Two legislative bodies must agree. As a counterweight to this legislative power, the President must sign the bill to make it law, and he or she also has the power to veto any proposed bill (Article I, Section 7). Finally, to complete the circle, Congress can override that presidential veto with a two-thirds vote (Article I, Section 7).

Congress creates the law, but it does not have the power to enforce the laws it passes. That is left to the Executive Branch. Yet the Executive Branch acts only with the financial resources provided and collected by Congress (Article I, Section 8). Congress controls the "purse strings," and thus keeps a measure of accountability over the Executive Branch.

In terms of running the government, the President appoints Executive Branch positions like Cabinet Members or Ambassadors. However, Congress retains the power to approve some Executive Branch appointments (Article II, Section 2). A similar balance happens with the armed forces. Congress retains the specific power to declare war (Article I, Section 8), but the President is the Commander in Chief and can control the direction of any war (Article II, Section 2).

The Executive appoints the federal judiciary and can pardon anyone sentenced by those judges (Article II, Section 2). The Legislative Branch retains the power to approve all federal judges, to set courts inferior to the Supreme Court (essentially creating the entire federal judicial system), and to set the jurisdiction of the courts (Article III, Section 1). At the same time, the Judicial Branch retains the power to review legislative and executive acts.

In terms of direct checks on power, the Legislative Branch maintains the power to impeach the President

(Article II, Section 4) and conduct the impeachment trial in the Senate (Article I, Section 3). The Legislative Branch can also impeach judges and conduct the impeachment trial in the Senate (Article I, Section 3).

These interconnected powers exist as a source of freedom that works in practice. As the Supreme Court once stated, "While the Constitution diffuses power the better to secure liberty, it also contemplates that practice will integrate the dispersed powers into a workable government. It enjoins upon its branches separateness but interdependence, autonomy but reciprocity."[34] This brief overview of interconnected power sources and mechanisms of oversight leaves little room to debate the Founders' intention to prevent concentrated power and establish a government ultimately accountable to the people. It recognizes an aspiration for control by the people—just like the jury.

Why Accountability Matters
The Verdict

Criminal trials generate dramatic tension. Two lawyers battle witness by witness, argument by argument, to convince a jury of the rightness of their cause. For the parties not privy to the deliberations in the jury room, there is no more heart-stopping moment than the announcement of the verdict. The foreperson stands up. A hush fills the room. Usually, jurors keep their facial expressions impassive, although occasionally a smile or tear betrays them. Then the judge turns to the foreperson and asks, "Has the jury reached a verdict?" When the foreperson responds, "Yes," everything stops and all eyes turn toward the jury.

The verdict is the final answer—a resolution to the problem that shattered the community order. It represents the moment of accountability. Derived from French and Latin, the word "verdict" means "to say the truth" or "a true saying." But in a constitutional sense, there is a different truth at issue. In the adversarial system, the truth gets measured against the standards of proof and legal instructions given to jurors. It is not about the facts of the world outside, but what evidence was produced in court. Other legal systems have chosen to adopt an inquisitorial system, where judges act as prosecutors as well as fact finders to investigate the witnesses and the case. The American choice of an adversarial process with a jury took a different path. We do not ask jurors to investigate the truth, but instead to evaluate the evidence against the standards of proof.

This result is not always satisfactory for jurors, who like most curious people want to find out "what actually happened."[35] Countless times, jurors have asked me after a case about "what really happened," "what was kept from them," or "what the lawyers knew." Many times my answers are not very satisfying, because usually the lawyers do not know that much more than the jury. Real-world situations are complicated and unclear, and both sides are usually well convinced of their version by the time they get to trial. The few cases that reach trial and are not settled by a plea agreement or financial settlement really do have contested facts.[36] Many times it is just not possible to find out what really happened. While on occasion evidence is suppressed in advance of trial, or facts are kept from a jury so as not to undermine the jury's impartial view of the case, most of the time the gaps in evidence are just gaps because of the way the facts were developed or what witnesses or evidence could be found.

In fact, while emotionally unsatisfying, the burdens of proof are supposed to lessen the burden of judgment for jurors. Instead of being weighted with the sometimes impossible task of figuring out what really happened, jurors are asked only to measure the evidence produced against the standard of proof. In criminal cases, prosecutors have a job to do, and most welcome the burden.

They are bringing their case because they believe in the evidence. The jury, then, merely evaluates what the government has produced and decides whether the evidence is convincing beyond a reasonable doubt. The jury acts "as a circuit breaker in the State's machinery of justice."[37] It holds the state accountable for trying to take the life or liberty of an individual.

At the same time, the jury acts as the community conscience, holding the defendant—a fellow community member—accountable for his or her criminal actions. As Judge David Bazelon once stated, "The very essence of the jury's function is its role as spokesman for the community conscience in determining whether or not blame can be imposed."[38] Juries are "instruments of public justice."[39] A jury's condemnation of an individual carries greater weight because it comes from the same community. A verdict symbolically represents the community view.[40]

Ordinary Gatekeepers

You are the law. As sworn members of a jury panel, you are asked to apply the law. This delegation of power means that jurors balance the values and standards in the law. You act as a mediating body of ordinary people, decentralized from the governing structure. Jurors take on their role as decision makers without any professional or economic bias toward the parties.[41]

In civil cases this can be a very important role. Take, for example, the determination of "negligence." In a civil case, the jury must determine whether an individual failed to use "ordinary care," defined as the care a reasonable person would have used under the circumstances of the case.[42] But what do the words "ordinary" or "reasonable" mean in the circumstances of a case? It presents a difficult judgment call, which we leave to jurors.

As an example of this type of case, imagine the following scenario: Main Street, USA. It is early in the morning and a woman is walking quickly to the gym. In the dark, she trips on a slab of raised concrete that has become dislodged from the sidewalk. She falls hard and injures her face. She sues the city for failing to fix the defect in the sidewalk that caused her injury. She demands compensation for her medical injuries as well as money damages for her pain and suffering.[43]

This case, like thousands of similar cases, actually happened. It is the grist of the civil tort mill. It was also a case that had an unlikely juror—a law professor who specialized in these types of tort cases, and who detailed his observations of ordinary, nonprofessional jurors sitting in judgment.[44] As the professor describes it, the case was one of negligence.[45] Should the city be held responsible for the woman's injuries? On one side of the equation, there was a defect in the sidewalk. Weeds and grass had grown around it, making it hard to see. The city had no systemic inspection program for sidewalks, but as a matter of policy this type of defect would have been repaired if reported. The woman had been injured, with close to $13,000 in medical bills plus lost wages and pain and suffering.[46] On the other side of the equation, the city had nearly two thousand miles of sidewalk under its control. No one had complained before, and the slab was 1.5 inches high. The place in which the woman had stumbled was busy with thousands of people using it on a daily basis. Further, the woman had hit her face in a way that meant that she didn't do anything to break her fall. The woman testified. Experts testified. City workers testified. The lawyers argued.[47] What is ordinary care? What is reasonable?

The case itself was dismissed before the verdict, but undeterred, the professor reconvened the jury to figure out how ordinary citizens would decide the case. The professor wanted to test whether his scholarly views on tort law would match the views of the jurors—regular people that included a grandmotherly trucker, an environmentalist, and a clerk who worked in a book-store. His experiment was revealing. First, the jurors observed facts missed by the lawyers. In photographs that had been submitted as evidence, the jurors noticed that the area around the contested sidewalk had been recently repaired, thus putting the city on constructive notice of the defect.[48] This fact had been overlooked by the lawyers in trial, but it could be seen in the photographs and was proof that the city was negligent. Yet, despite this clear notice, the jury could not get past the credibility of the woman in the case. None of the jury members could understand how someone could fall on their face and not catch themselves before they hit the sidewalk.[49] Eventually, the jury determined that the woman was "contributorily negligent," meaning that she failed to take care of her own safety. The result would have meant a loss for the woman and a denial of any damages.

From the torts professor's perspective, the legal issue was more complex. He didn't subscribe to the belief that the failure to stop the fall was an act of contributory negligence. Maybe this failure should lessen the damages, but it should not deny the plaintiff all relief.[50] As a torts expert, the professor was likely right. However, as a juror, he understood that the balancing of interests might cut against the woman. He also recognized that throughout the trial the credibility assessments of the jurors flatly contradicted his own.[51] Jurors liked witnesses he hated, and credited witnesses he dismissed. What ordinary people thought was, not surprisingly, not the same as what a law professor thought. Yet in the end, the professor recognized the value of having ordinary people, not legal experts, come to a final resolution of the problem. Jurors came to a reasonable decision about what was reasonable.

A Community Judgment

Many times after sitting and talking with a jury that has reached a verdict in a criminal case, one is struck by the powerful notion of "common sense" that pervades the jury room. It has been said that "[t]welve jurors know more of the common affairs of life than does one man, and they can draw wiser and safer conclusions than a single judge."[52] Of course, common sense is not really a legal principle, and it is hard to figure out what jurors mean by it in a criminal context. But they say it time after time: "We just sort of thought it made sense to us," or "We just applied common sense." Analyzed properly, I think it means that the jurors infused their legal judgment with nonlawyer values, coming up with a fair solution to the problem presented. Judge William Young once wrote, "The American jury 'must rank as a daring effort in human arrangement to work out a solution to the tensions between law and equity and anarchy.' No other legal institution sheds greater insight into the character of American justice."[53]

Judge Young's comment underscores another angle of what we mean by accountability. Sometimes, accountability doesn't require holding someone completely responsible, but means accounting for a fair result. We allow jurors to make the hard calls to balance law and fairness. This is not a weakness in the jury system, but rather the reason for the jury system. Ironically, sometimes the jury can be the release valve of justice, by judging accountability without really being held accountable itself. As Judge Learned Hand recognized:

> The institution of trial by jury—especially in criminal cases—has its hold upon public favor chiefly for two reasons. The individual can forfeit his liberty—to say nothing of his life—only at the hands of those who,

unlike any official, are in no wise accountable, directly or indirectly, for what they do, and who at once separate and melt anonymously in the community from which they came. Moreover, since if they acquit their verdict is final, no one is likely to suffer of whose conduct they do not morally disapprove; and this introduces a slack into the enforcement of law, tempering its rigor by the mollifying influence of current ethical considerations. . . . This power to issue an unreviewable general verdict despite the letter of the law introduces a critical check on the government before it can impose criminal punishment and provides a mechanism for correcting overinclusive general criminal laws.[54]

How can accountability be had by people who are not really accountable for their actions? First, jurors are accountable because they are making a representative decision for their community in their community. If they let a polluter or drug dealer go free, they live with that decision in their neighborhoods. Second, jurors can balance the harm done in a way that is closer to a community sense of fairness. It is no secret to say jurors sometimes compromise in their verdicts—sometimes fairly, sometimes not. Yet that compromise is an accounting—a measure of wrong done to harm done, as viewed by community representatives.

I have spoken to jurors who have candidly admitted to horse-trading different charges in the jury room in order to reach a final verdict, as well as to jurors who refused to compromise. I have spoken to jurors who came out with their own legal and moral balance that was wholly independent (and counter) to the arguments of both the prosecution and defense. And I have spoken to jurors who arrived at balanced decisions (for both convictions and acquittals) based on common sense and a legally accurate interpretation of the law. While I have been alternatively troubled, puzzled, and pleased by the various methods of reaching a verdict, it is part of a human process of decision making, and one that has a long history in our justice system.

Our laws "purport to be based on the collective values of the community."[55] Jurors take those collective values written in law and look at an individual case and an individual person. Since it is the community values that have been broken, it is the community that judges the damage done and the accountability that is necessary.[56] This is a different perspective than if they were to look at the law as voters. An overly broad law might make perfect sense in the abstract, but not in actual application.[57] For example, we might all support a law that criminalizes having illegal drugs in a house with young children present. We might all want those who were aware of the drugs to be punished. But if a jury is faced with a father, a mother, a grandmother, and several teenage boys who might all have known about the drugs in the house, it might also ascribe different levels of culpability to each of the parties. A jury might weigh the same evidence differently depending on the individual—a hardworking grandmother or a strung-out mother—under consideration. This does not mean that a jury should ignore the law, but from experience, most juries would take an individualized approach to each of the accused.

Balancing law and equity presents a difficult and potentially dangerous result. In some cases, jury equity spills over to jury lawlessness. This is what Judge Young meant by the potential for "anarchy." Jury lawlessness (sometimes called "jury nullification") exists where jurors consciously ignore the law to reach a verdict. While jury lawlessness has always been a part of our history, it is not a comfortable history. For every anti-tyranny jury verdict like John Peter Zenger's or the juries that refused to convict abolitionists prosecuted under the Fugitive Slave Act, there have been thousands of less idealistic outcomes. For almost two centuries in the South, people of color were denied full justice because a narrow-minded, race-based community conscience refused to convict white citizens for crimes against minorities, or equally troubling, juries convicted minorities for crimes in the face of evidence of innocence.[58] Jury power unbounded by the law undermines the rule of law.

To resolve the tension between law, equity, and anarchy, one must go back to the dual accountability of the jury. The moral authority of a conviction rests in its connection to the community. The reason why a society accepts the convictions of individuals as "just" is because it trusts that the same system can produce acquittals. Or to put it another way, because we trust that juries will follow the law to acquit, when they convict, we know that the judgment can be trusted. Filtered through a system of common sense and common values, the jury process checks the parties and the system. Again, as Judge Young wrote, "[j]urors bring their good sense and practical knowledge into our courts. . . . The acceptability and moral authority of the justice provided in our courts rests in large part on the presence of the jury. It is through this process, in which the jury applies rules formulated in light of common experience to the facts of each case that we deliver the best justice our society knows how to provide."[59] In this way, your verdict holds the judicial system and the parties accountable.

Is it a perfect system? No. But it represents one of the most effective ways to infuse democratic and community accountability into a process of decision making. No wonder then that 90 percent of state and federal judges believed that properly selected juries were conscientious, understood the legal issues, and reached just and fair verdicts.[60] And tellingly, 80 percent of those same judges said that if charged with a crime they would rather have a jury decide the case over a judge. The number was slightly lower in civil cases, with 60 percent of judges (still a majority) choosing a jury over a judge.[61] As a means of accountability, juries thus represent a very successful experiment in democratic judgment.

I'm no idealist to believe firmly in the integrity of our courts and in the jury system—that is no ideal to me, it is a living, working reality. . . . A court is no better than each . . . of you sitting before me on this jury. A court is only as sound as its jury, and a jury is only as sound as the people who make it up.
—Harper Lee, *To Kill a Mockingbird*

United States Post Office (n.d., ca. 1897) Completed in 1897
SUPERVISING ARCHITECTS: Willoughby J. Edbrooke, Jeremiah O'Rourke, and William Martin Aiken
The Untied States District Court for the Eastern District of Louisiana met here until 1933; the United States Circuit Court for the Eastern District of Louisiana met here until that court was abolished in 1912. Now the City Club of Baton Rouge.

SOURCE: NATIONAL ARCHIVES, RG 121-C, BOX 13, FOLDER H, PRINT 3

Conclusion

In the local courthouse, 4:30 p.m. is known as "the witching hour" for jury verdicts. A half an hour more and the jury will need to return for another day of deliberations.

I look across at my young client still wringing his hands. He has barely moved from our uncomfortable bench for three days. The courthouse feels empty. A law clerk shuffling papers in the hallway interrupts the stifling silence. I touch my copy of the Constitution for good luck. Will the jury be willing to come back for yet another day of deliberations?

The courtroom clerk pokes her head out into the hallway. "We have a verdict," she announces. My heart beats louder in my chest. I watch my client ease himself off the bench. He neither smiles nor frowns and heads to take his seat in courtroom. He looks to be at peace. Watching him, I wonder if he knows that he could be taking his last few breaths as a free man. I wonder if he has any idea of the trust he, and all of us, have placed in twelve strangers.

That moment of worry and faith encapsulates the importance of the jury. If we did not believe in the system of rights, responsibilities, and duties under the Constitution, we would not be willing to enter that courtroom. But we do.

The faith to walk through those doors, trusting that twelve citizens will do the hard work to reach a fair verdict, is one of the greatest tributes to the jury system. It happens every day, all across the United States. It happens in the most trivial of cases and the most serious. It is why ordinary Americans trust the system of justice.

Even before America was America, juries represented the responsibilities and ideals of citizenship. One cannot find a more honorable lineage than a tradition that dates from the first colony at Jamestown, to the Declaration of Independence, through the Constitution and the Bill of Rights, to the present day. It is our heritage, and a proud one. Every day since that time, people just like you have gotten up, gone to court, and turned from an ordinary citizen into a constitutional citizen.

Jury duty represents one of our finest forms of civic engagement. We transform ourselves into constitutional actors. We practice the constitutional values etched in the Constitution even if we do not always recognize the connection. Your service is an example of the values the Founders hoped would be woven into the fabric of the nation's civic life. Every time you serve as a juror, you become closer to this constitutional spirit; and every time you reflect on and appreciate these principles, you strengthen our constitutional character.

This book is but an expression of that character. Your work in the jury room and your presence at the courthouse is its fulfillment. From all of us who practice in criminal and civil court and try to live up to the constitutional values of a nation, thank you.

* * *

The values in this book are American values. They are not mere words, but rather demands for action. They are rooted in the text, history, and actions of our fellow citizens. They also require a future commitment. The hope is that this book presents a moment of focused attention on how constitutional rights affect your life in this country. Every morning under the inspiring facade of the local courthouse, you can see the flesh and blood embodiment of civic participation, deliberation, fairness, equality, liberty, accountability, freedom of conscience, and the common good. Waiting in line, dutiful citizens prepare themselves to become constitutional actors. But, of course, they need not wait for jury service. The values exist before and after your civic service. The relevance of those values exist today and every day. All you have to do is read the Constitution.

NOTES

Notes to the Foreword

1. For more information on this event and its effects, *see* Charles J. Ogletree Jr., *All Deliberate Speed: Reflections on the First Half Century of Brown v. Board of Education* (New York: Norton, 2004), 45–48.
2. Austin Sarat & Charles J. Ogletree Jr., *From Lynch Mob to the Killing State: Race and the Death Penalty in America* (Charles Hamilton Houston Institute Series on Race and Justice) (New York: New York University Press, 2006), 8, 150–51, 225–26.
3. *Hollins v. State of Oklahoma*, 295 U.S. 394, 395 (1935). *See* Paul Finkelman, "Not Only the Judges Robes Were Black: African American Lawyers as Social Engineers," 47 Stan. L. Rev. 161, 187 (1994).
4. 407 U.S. 493, 502 (1972).
5. *See* Justice Marshall's concurring opinion in *Batson v. Kentucky,* 476 U.S. 79 (1986): "The decision today will not end the racial discrimination that peremptories inject into the jury selection process. That goal can be accomplished only by eliminating peremptory challenges entirely." *See also* Charles

J. Ogletree Jr., "Just Say No! A Proposal to Eliminate Racially Discriminatory Uses of Peremptory Challenges," 31 Am. Crim. L. Rev. 1099 (1994).

6. Earl Caldwell, "Angela Davis Acquitted on All Charges," New York Times (June 5, 1972).

7. G. K. Chesterton, *Tremendous Trifles*, "The Twelve Men" (New York: Dodd, Mead, 1920), 87–88. The quote is from the original source. Judge Arnason took some minor liberties with the text. *See* Caldwell, "Angela Davis Acquitted on All Charges," for the original transcript at the Davis trial.

Notes to the Introduction

1. William Powers, "Put Up Your Dukes," The Atlantic, July 4, 2006.

2. *Texas v. Johnson*, 491 U.S. 397 (1989).

3. Rachel E. Barkow, "Recharging the Jury: The Criminal Jury's Constitutional Role in an Era of Mandatory Sentencing," 152 U. Pa. L. Rev. 33, 54 (2003), *citing* William E. Nelson, *Americanization of the Common Law: The Impact of Legal Change on Massachusetts Society, 1760–1830* (Georgia: Georgia University Press, 1994), 96.

4. Albert Alschuler & Andrew Deiss, "A Brief History of Criminal Jury in the United States," 61 U. Chi. L. Rev. 867, 870, n.15 (1994); "Development in the Law: The Civil Jury: IV: Unshrinking the Federal Civil Jury," 110 Harv. L. Rev. 1466, 1468 (1997).

5. The Declaration of Independence, para. 20 (U.S. 1776).

6. Alschuler & Deiss, "A Brief History," 61 U. Chi. L. Rev. at 869–70. *See also* Lisa Litwiller, "Has the Supreme Court Sounded the Death Knell for Jury-Assessed Punitive Damages? A Critical Re-examination of the American Jury," 36 U.S.F. L. Rev. 411 (2002).

7. Leonard W. Levy, *Origins of the Bill of Rights* (New Haven: Yale University Press 1999), 227.

8. Alschuler & Deiss, "A Brief History," 61 U. Chi. L. Rev. at 870.

9. U.S. Const., amend. V, VI, VII.

10. Akhil Reed Amar, "Reinventing Juries: Ten Suggested Ideas," 28 U.C. Davis L. Rev. 1169, 1170 (1995) ("[T]he 'no prior restraint' doctrine that intertwined with freedom of the press had its deepest roots in jury trial ideas. A prior restraint could issue from a judge via an injunction, and have bite in contempt proceedings that excluded a jury; nonprior restraints,

like libel judgments, could have bite only if the government could persuade a jury of the publisher's peers to rule against him."); Stephen A. Siegel, "Injunctions for Defamation, Juries, and the Clarifying Lens of 1868," 56 Buff. L. Rev. 655, 664–70 (2008); Michael I. Meyerson, "The Neglected History of the Prior Restraint Doctrine: Rediscovering the Link Between the First Amendment and the Separation of Powers," 34 Ind. L. Rev. 295, 321 (2001); Akhil Reed Amar, "The Bill of Rights as a Constitution," 100 Yale L.J. 1131, 1150 (1991).

11. Amar, "The Bill of Rights," 100 Yale L.J. at 1179–80.
12. Amar, "Reinventing Juries," 28 U.C. Davis L. Rev. at 1170–72.
13. *See also United States v. Kandirakis*, 441 F. Supp. 2d 282, 309–15 (D. Mass 2006).
14. Gregory E. Mize, Paula L. Hannaford-Agor, & Nicole Waters, *The State of the States Survey of Jury Improvement Efforts*, National Center for State Courts, Executive Summary, at 2 (2010). NCSC statistics estimate that annually there are 148,558 state jury trials, 5,940 federal jury trials, with 1,526,520 citizens actually impaneled.
15. *Id.* NSSC estimates that there were approximately 31,857,797 summons mailed, reaching 14.8% of the adult population.
16. *Id.* at 3.
17. American Bar Association, *Perceptions of the U.S. Justice System* 63 (1998), *available at* http://www.abanow.org/wordpress/wp-content/files_flutter/1269460858_20_1_1_7_Upload_File.pdf.
18. William L. Dwyer, *In the Hands of the People: The Trial Jury's Origins, Triumphs, Troubles, and Future in American Democracy* (New York: Thomas Dunne, St. Martin's Press, 2002), 153.
19. *See, for example*, Lisa Lee Mancini Harden, "The End of the Peremptory Challenge? The Implications of J. E. B. v. Alabama ex rel. T. B. for Jury Selection in Alabama," 47 Ala. L. Rev. 243, 247–57 (1995); Jeffrey S. Brand, "The Supreme Court, Equal Protection, and Jury Selection: Denying that Race Still Matters," 1994 Wis. L. Rev. 511 (1994); Douglas L. Colbert, "Challenging the Challenge: Thirteenth Amendment as a Prohibition Against the Racial Use of Peremptory Challenges," 76 Cornell L. Rev. 1, 13–32 (1990).
20. Sandra D. Jordan, "The Criminal Trial Jury: Erosion of Jury Power," 5 How. Scroll Soc. J. Rev. 1, 45–57 (2002); Lawrence M. Friedman, "Some Notes on the Civil Jury in Historical Perspective" 48 DePaul L. Rev. 201, 213–19 (1998); Andrew

G. Deiss, "Comment, Negotiating Justice: The Criminal Trial Jury in a Pluralist America," 3 U. Chi. L. Sch. Roundtable 323, n.144 (1996).

21. Graham C. Lilly, "The Decline of the American Jury," 72 U. Colo. L. Rev. 53, 83–89 (2003); Mark Cammack, "In Search of the Post-Positivist Jury," 70 Ind. L. Rev. 405, 405–9 (1995); James C. Oldham, "The Origins of the Special Jury," 50 U. Chi. L. Rev. 137 (1983).

Notes to Chapter 1

1. The federal government bans felons from jury service. Other jurisdictions ban felons for a period of time after they have served their sentence. *See* Neil Vidmar & Valerie P. Hans, *American Juries: The Verdict* (Amherst, NY: Prometheus, 2007), 80; Brian C. Kalt, "The Exclusion of Felons from Jury Service," 53 Am. U. L. Rev. 65 (2003).

2. Vikram David Amar, "Jury Service as Political Participation Akin to Voting," 80 Cornell L. Rev. 203, 253–54 (1995).

3. Gregory E. Mize, Paula L. Hannaford-Agor, & Nicole Waters, *The State of the States Survey of Jury Improvement Efforts*, National Center for State Courts, Executive Summary, at 2 (2010).

4. Robert G. Boatright, "Why Citizens Don't Respond to Jury Summonses, and What Courts Can Do About It," 82 Judicature 156, 158–69 (1999).

5. *See* Roi Holt, Janvier Slick, & Amy Rayborn, "Understanding Jurors," 63 JUL Or. St. B. Bull. 17, 18 (2003).

6. Arthur Santana, "D.C. to Jurors: Show Up or Else; Court Issues 187 Arrest Warrants for Residents Who Ignored Summons," Washington Post (Dec. 25, 2001), at B1.

7. Jeffrey Abramson, *We the Jury: The Jury System and the Ideal of Democracy* (Cambridge: Harvard University Press, 2001), 249.

8. Nancy S. Marder, "Bringing Jury Instructions into the Twenty-First Century," 81 Notre Dame L. Rev., 449, 507 n.259 (2006).

9. Valerie P. Hans & Neil Vidmar, *Judging the Jury* (Cambridge, MA: Perseus, 1986), 114.

10. Bethany K. Dumas, "Jury Trials: Lay Jurors, Pattern Jury Instructions, and Comprehension Issues," 67 Tenn. L. Rev. 701, 705 (2000); *see also* Marder, "Bringing Jury Instructions into the Twenty-First Century," 81 Notre Dame L. at 454–58; Peter Tiersma, "The Rocky Road to Legal Reform: Improving

the Language of Jury Instructions," 66 Brook. L. Rev. 1081,
1101–10 (2001).

11. All textual references are from the United States Archives
original version. In the text, the capitalization of certain
words has been modified for the reader.

12. President Abraham Lincoln, The Gettysburg Address (Nov.
19, 1863).

13. Kelly Nickles, ed., *Pocket Patriot: Quotes from American Heroes*
(Cincinnati: Writer's Digest Books, 2005), 34.

14. B. Michael Dunn, "Learning Lessons and Speaking Rights:
Creating Educated and Democratic Juries," 68 Ind. L.J. 1229,
1232 (1993).

15. Robert W. Sheef, "Note 'Public Citizens' and the Constitution:
Bridging the Gap Between Popular Sovereignty and Original
Intent," 69 Fordham L. Rev. 2201, n.28, n.47 (2001).

16. Rachel Barkow, "Recharging the Jury: The Criminal Jury's
Constitutional Role in an Era of Mandatory Sentencing," 152
U. Pa. L. Rev. 33, 53 (2003).

17. Abramson, *supra* at 23–24.

18. Alschuler, "A Brief History," 61 U. Chi. L. Rev. at 871–74; *see
also* John D. Jackson, "Making Juries Accountable," 50 Am. J.
Comp. L. 477, 506–8 (2002); Frederick Schauer, "The Role of
the People in First Amendment Theory," 74 Cal. L. Rev. 761,
761–65 (1986).

19. Alschuler, "A Brief History," 61 U. Chi. L. Rev. at 874–75.

20. Douglas G. Smith, "The Historical and Constitutional Contexts of Jury Reform," 25 Hofstra L. Rev. 377, 424 (1996).

21. David McCullough, *John Adams* (New York: Simon & Schuster, 2001), 65.

22. Andrea McArdle, "Race and the American Originary
Moment: The Boston Massacre Narratives and the Idea of
Citizenship," 7 Rutgers Race & L. Rev. 51, 57–58 (2005). *See
also* McCullough, *supra* at 65–66.

23. Akhil Reed Amar, *America's Constitution: A Biography* (New
York: Random House, 2005), 237.

24. McCullough, *supra* at 68.

25. *Id.*

26. Amar, *supra* at 237.

27. Ric Simmons, "Re-examining the Grand Jury: Is There Room
for Democracy in the Criminal Justice System?" 82 B.U. L.
Rev. 1, 12–13 (2002); *see also Jones v. Unites States*, 526 U.S. 227,
246–47 (1999).

28. Simmons, "Re-examining the Grand Jury," 82 B.U. L. Rev. at 1–12; Matthew P. Harrington, "The Law-Finding Function of the American Jury," 1999 Wis. L. Rev. 377, 386 (1999), *citing* William E. Nelson, *The Americanization of the Common Law: The Impact of Legal Change on Massachusetts Society, 1760–1830* (Cambridge: Harvard University Press 1994), 15; and *Township of Fallowfield v. Township of Marlborogh*, 1 Dall. 29 (Pa. 1776) (appeal of sessions court order removing a pauper from town).

29. Simmons, "Re-examining the Grand Jury," 82 B.U. L. Rev. at 1–12.

30. Leonard W. Levy, *Origins of the Bill of Rights* (New Haven: Yale University Press, 1999), n.7, at 221.

31. Akhil Reed Amar, *The Bill of Rights: Creation and Reconstruction* (New Haven: Yale University Press, 1998), 94–95.

32. *Blakely v. Washington*, 542 U.S. 296, 306 (2004), *citing* Letter XV by Federal Farmer (January 18, 1788), *reprinted in* 2 *The Complete Anti-Federalist* 315, 320 (H. Storing, ed.) (Chicago: University of Chicago Press, 1981).

33. *See* Amar, "Jury Service as Political Participation," 80 Cornell L. Rev. at 222–41; Robert J. Kaczorowski, "Federal Enforcement of Civil Rights During the First Reconstruction," 23 Fordham Urb. L.J. 155 (1995).

34. Reva B. Siegel, "She the People: The Nineteenth Amendment, Sex Equality, Federalism, and the Family," 115 Harv. L. Rev. 947, 968–76 (2002); Gretchen Ritter, "Jury Service and Women's Citizenship Before and After the Nineteenth Amendment," 20 Law & Hist. Rev. 479, 497–500 (2002); JoEllen Lind, "Dominance and Democracy: The Legacy of Woman Suffrage for the Voting Right," 5 UCLA Women's L.J. 103, 126–38 (1994).

35. Amar, "Jury Service as Political Participation," 80 Cornell L. Rev. at 218, *quoting* Representative Fascell, 108 Cong. Rec. 17,657 (1962) (remarks of Rep. Fascell).

36. Steven Ramirez & Aliza Organick, "Taking Voting Rights Seriously: Race and the Integrity of Democracy in America," N. Ill. U. L. Rev. 427, 441 (2007); Gregory A. Loken, "Gratitude and the Map of Moral Duties Toward Children," 31 Ariz. St. L.J. 1121, 1197 (1999).

37. *Whitney v. California*, 274 U.S. 357, 375 (1927) (Brandies, J., concurring).

38. Akhil Reed Amar, "The Bill of Rights as a Constitution," 100 Yale L.J. 1131, 1161 (1991).

39. Frances Fitzgerald, "Annals of Religion: Come One, Come All," The New Yorker, Dec. 3, 2007, at 46.

40. *Parker v. District of Columbia*, 478 F.3d 370, 386–89 (D.C. Cir. 2007).

41. Douglas G. Smith, "Structural and Functional Aspects of the Jury: Comparative Analysis and Proposals for Reform," 48 Ala. L. Rev. 441, 480–81 (1997), *citing* Alexis de Tocqueville, *Democracy in America, Vol. 1* (Phillips Bradley, ed., 1945) (New York: Vintage, 1990), 284–85.

42. *Powers v. Ohio*, 499 U.S. 400, 407 (1991); *see also J. E. B. v. Alabama ex rel. T. B.*, 511 U.S. 127, 153 (1994).

43. Amar, "Jury Service as Political Participation," 80 Cornell L. Rev. at 221, *citing* Alexis de Tocqueville, *Democracy in America* (J. P. Mayer & Max Lerner eds., George Lawrence trans., 1966) (New York: Anchor, 1969), 276.

44. Henry Kalven Jr. & Hans Zeisel, *The American Jury* (Chicago: University of Chicago 1966), 3–4.

45. Marder, "Bringing Jury Instructions into the Twenty-First Century," 81 Notre Dame L. Rev. at 451.

46. Tocqueville (Bradley, ed.), *supra* at 285.

47. Amar, *supra* at 93.

48. John Gastil, E. Pierre Deess, Philip J. Weiser, & Cindy Simmons, *The Jury and Democracy: How Jury Deliberation Promotes Civic Engagement and Political Participation* (New York: Oxford University Press, 2010), 108.

49. *Id.*

50. American Bar Association, *Jury Service: Is Fulfilling Your Civic Duty a Trial?* (July 2004), *available at* http://www.abanow.org/wordpress/wp-content/files_flutter/1272052715_20_1_1_7_Upload_File.pdf.

51. *Alvarado v. State*, 486 P. 2d 891, 903–4 (Alaska 1971), *quoting Ballard v. United States*, 329 U.S. 187, 195 (1946).

52. Amar, *America's Constitution: A Biography*, at 5.

53. Amar, "The Bill of Rights as a Constitution," 100 Yale L.J. at 1152.

54. Amar, *supra* at 236.

Notes to Chapter 2

1. Stephan Landsman, "The Civil Jury in America: Scenes from an Unappreciated History," 44 Hastings L.J. 579, 584 (1993).

2. R. J. Farley, "Instructions to Juries: Their Role in the Judicial Process," 42 Yale L.J. 194, 196 (1934).

3. *Id.* at 200; Shari Seidman Diamond & Neil Vidmar, "Jury Room Ruminations on Forbidden Topics," 87 Va. L. Rev. 1857, 1857 (2001).

4. Landsman, "The Civil Jury in America," 44 Hastings L.J. at 586.

5. Neil Vidmar & Valerie P. Hans, *American Juries: The Verdict* (Amherst, NY: Prometheus, 2007), at 66.

6. *Taylor v. Louisiana*, 419 U.S. 522, 528 (1975); *see also Tennessee v. Lane*, 541 U.S. 509, 523 (2004); *J. E. B. v. Alabama ex rel. T. B.*, 511 U.S. 127, 134 (1994).

7. *Duren v. Missouri*, 439 U.S. 357, 364 (1979).

8. *Taylor v. Louisiana*, 419 U.S. at 530.

9. *Peters v. Kiff*, 407 U.S. 493, 501 (1972), *citing In re Murchison*, 349 U.S. 133, 136 (1955) ("A fair trial in a fair tribunal is a basic requirement of due process."); *Tumey v. Ohio*, 273, U.S. 510 (1927).

10. Valerie P. Hans & Alayna Jehle, "Avoid Bald Men and People with Green Socks? Other Ways to Improve the Voir Dire Process in Jury Selection," 78 Chi.-Kent L. Rev. 1179, 1180 (2003), *citing* Michael J. Saks, "What Do Jury Experiments Tell Us About How Juries (Should) Make Decisions?," 6 S. Cal. Interdisc. L.J. 1 (1997); *see also Wainwright v. Witt*, 469 U.S. 412, n.11 (1985) ("[N]umerous studies have all but confirmed that death-qualified juries are conviction-prone.").

11. Vidmar & Hans, *supra* at 87 (which also locates the root of the word in French, "to see them say").

12. *See* American Bar Association, *Principles for Juries and Jury Trials*, Principle 7, Courts Should Protect Juror Privacy Insofar as Consistent with the Requirements of Justice and the Public Interest, at 35 (August 2005), *available at* http://www.americanbar.org/content/dam/aba/migrated/juryprojectstandards/principles.authcheckdam.pdf.

13. Stephanie Leonard Yarbrough, "The Jury Consultant: Friend or Foe of Justice," 54 SMU L. Rev. 1885, 1886–87 (2001).

14. Barbara Allen Babcock, "A Place in the Palladium: Women's Rights and Jury Service," 61 U. Cin. L. Rev. 1139, 1145 (1993).

15. Vidmar & Hans, *supra* at 89; *see also* Lance Pugmire & Steve Henson, "Bryant Jurors' Bias Becomes Issue," Los Angeles Times (Sept. 1, 2004).

16. Vidmar & Hans, *supra* at 89.

17. Gregory E. Mize, "On Better Jury Selection: Spotting UFO Jurors Before They Enter the Jury Room," 3 Ct. Rev. 10, 10–15 (1999).

18. Oregon State Bar Bulletin February/March 2006 (Oregon State Bar), 56 Or. St. B. Bull. 7.

19. J. Walter Sinclair, Mark A. Behrens, & Cary Silverman, "Making Jury Duty a Little Friendlier," 46-OCT Advocate (Idaho) 23 (2003).

20. Paul W. Rebein, Victor E. Schwartz, & Cary Silverman, "Jury (Dis)Service: Why People Avoid Jury Duty and What Florida Can Do About It," 28 Nova L. Rev. 143, 143 (2003); Graham C. Lilly, "The Decline of the American Jury," 72 U. Colo. L. Rev. 53, 61–63 (2001); Thomas L. Fowler, "Filling the Box: Responding to Jury Duty Avoidance," 23 N.C. Cent. L.J. 1 (1997/1998).

21. Craig T. Enoch & David F. Johnson, "Narrowing the Ability to Strike Jurors: The Texas Supreme Court Addresses Important Voir Dire Issues," 39 Tex. Tech L. Rev. 229, 229–30 (2007).

22. *United States v. Kandirakis*, 441 F. Supp. 2d 282, 316 (D. Mass. 2006), *citing Coffin v. United States*, 156 U.S. 432, 454 (1895), *citing* 4 William Blackstone, Commentaries at 358.

23. Diamond & Vidmar, "Jury Room Ruminations," 87 Va. L. Rev. at 1859. *See also* James P. Thomas, "Constitutional Law—Sixth Amendment—Juror Misconduct—Premature Deliberations," 32 Duq. L. Rev. 983 (1994).

24. *Crawford v. Washington*, 541 U.S. 36, 61 (2004).

25. *Id.* at 44.

26. *Id.*, *citing* 1 D. Jardine, *Criminal Trials* 435 (1832).

27. *Crawford v. Washington*, 541 U.S. 36 (2004).

28. *Duncan v. Louisiana*, 391 U.S. 145, 149 (1968).

29. George Anastaplo, "Constitutionalism, Rule of Rules: Explorations," 39 Brandeis L.J. 17 (2000); Jack M. Balkin, "Original Meaning and Constitutional Redemption," 24 Const. Commentary 427, 429 (2007); Paul E. McGreal, "Ambition's Playground," 68 Fordham L. Rev. 1107, 1167–71 (2000).

30. *Harris v. Nelson*, 394 U.S. 286, 290–91 (1969).

31. Leonard Levy, *Origins of the Bill of Rights* (New Haven: Yale University Press, 2001), 68.

32. *Id.* at 71.

33. Akhil Reed Amar, *America's Constitution: A Biography* (New York: Random House, 2005), at 124–25.

34. Landsman, "The Civil Jury in America," 44 Hastings L.J. at 598–99.

35. *Id.* at 597.

36. Shirley S. Abrahamson, "Justice and Juror," 20 Ga. L. Rev. 257, 278 (1986).

37. *Id.* at 277, *quoting* G. K. Chesterton, "The Twelve Men," in *Tremendous Trifles* 80, 85–86 (1909).

38. William L. Dwyer, *In the Hands of the People: The Trial Jury's Origins, Triumphs, Troubles, and Future in American Democracy* (New York: Thomas Dunne, St. Martin's Press, 2002), 16–17.

39. *Id.* at 29–30.

40. Judith L. Ritter, "Your Lips Are Moving . . . but the Words Aren't Clear: Dissecting the Presumption That Jurors Understand Instructions," 69 Mo. L. Rev. 163, 187–93 (2004); Patrick J. Kelley & Laurel A. Wendt, "What Judges Tell Juries About Negligence: A Review of Pattern Jury Instructions," 77 Chi.-Kent L. Rev. 587, 593–95 (2002); Peter Tiersma, "The Rocky Road to Legal Reform: Improving the Language of Jury Instructions," 66 Brook. L. Rev. 1081, 1083–84 (2001).

41. ABA American Jury Project Initiative, *available at* http://www.abavideonews.org/ABA294/.

42. *Id.*

43. *Marbury v. Madison*, 5 U.S. (1 Cranch) 137 (1803).

44. Thomas Jefferson, Letter to Joseph Priestly (June 12, 1802), in 8 *The Writings of Thomas Jefferson, Vol. X* (P. Ford ed., 1897) (Memorial Ed., 1907) (1905), 325, *cited* in Akhil Reed Amar, "The Bill of Rights as a Constitution," 100 Yale L.J. 1131, 1208 (1991).

45. *Green v. United States*, 356 U.S. 165, 215–16 (1958) (Black, J., dissenting).

46. *Melendez-Diaz v. Massachusetts*, 129 S. Ct. 2527, 2556 (2009) (Kennedy, J., dissenting); *Polk County v. Dodson*, 454 U.S. 312, 318 (1981) ("a defense lawyer best serves the public . . . by advancing the undivided interests of his client") (internal quotations omitted); Charles J. Ogletree Jr., "Beyond Justifications: Seeking Motivations to Sustain Public Defenders," 106 Harv. L. Rev. 1239, 1246–47 (1993); Abbe Smith, "Nice Work if You Can Get It: 'Ethical' Jury Selection in Criminal Defense," 67 Fordham L. Rev. 523, 563–67 (1998).

47. Melanie D. Wilson, "Prosecutor's 'Doing Justice' Through Osmosis: Reminders to Creating a Culture of Cooperation," 45 Am. J. Crim. L. Rev. 67, 81–87 (2008); Angela J. Davis, "The Legal Profession's Failure to Discipline Unethical Prosecutors," 36 Hofstra L. Rev. 275, 282–91 (2007); Fred A. Zacharias, "Structuring the Ethics of Prosecutorial Trial Practice: Can Prosecutor's Do Justice?" 44 Vand. L. Rev. 45 (1991); *United States v. Young*, 470 U.S. 1, 26 (1985) (Brennan, J., dissenting).

48. The Supreme Court oath reads, "I do solemnly swear (or affirm) that I will administer justice without respect to persons, and do equal right to the poor and to the rich, and that I will faithfully and impartially discharge and perform all the duties incumbent upon me as Justice under the Constitution and laws of the United States. So help me God." 28 U.S.C. § 453 (1990).

49. Megan Healy McClung, "A Brief History of the Jury," 19 MAR CBA Rec. 35, 36 (2005).

50. Maryam Ahranjani, Andrew G. Ferguson, & Jamin B. Raskin, *Youth Justice in America* (Washington, DC: CQ Press, 2005), 228–29.

51. Anthony Lewis, *Gideon's Trumpet* (New York: Vintage, 1989) (1964), 60–64.

52. *Korematsu v. United States*, 323 U.S. 214 (1944); *Scott v. Sanford*, 60 U.S. 393 (1857); U.S. Const. Art. I, § 2 (1787); *see also* Eric L. Miller, "Constitutional Conscience," 83 B.U. L. Rev. 1017 (2003).

53. Sara Mosle, "The Case of the Lone Star Witness," New York Times (Oct. 30, 2005); Paul Duggin, "Massive Drug Sweep Divides Texas Town; ACLU Sues as FBI Probes Black Prosecutions" Washington Post (Jan. 22, 2001).

54. Adam Liptak, "Texas Governor Pardons 35 Arrested in Tainted Sting," New York Times (Aug. 23, 2003).

Notes to Chapter 3

1. Benjamin Weiser, "Civic Duty, Sure, but Wasn't the White House Enough?" New York Times (March 1, 2003).

2. *Powers v. Ohio*, 499 U.S. 400, 409 (1991).

3. The *Powers* case applied the concept of "third party standing," by which third parties (Mr. Powers) could sue to challenge the exclusion of an African American venire person. *See, for example*, Nancy Marder, "Beyond Gender: Peremptory Challenges and the Roles of the Jury," 73 Texas L. Rev. 1041, 1116 (1995); Judge David Hittner & Eric J. R. Nichols, "Jury Selection in Federal Civil Litigation: General Procedures, New Rules, and the Arrival of Batson," 23 Tex. Tech. L. Rev. 407, 460 (1992).

4. *Batson v. Kentucky*, 476 U.S. 79, 82 (1986).

5. *Id.* at 82–84.

6. *Id.* at 86, *quoting Strauder v. West Virginia*, 100 U.S. 303, 306 (1880).

7. *Id.* at 87 (emphasis added).

8. *Id.* at 100.

9. *Powers*, 499 U.S. at 402.

10. *Id.* at 409.

11. *Id.* at 416.

12. *Georgia v. McCollum*, 505 U.S. 42 (1992).

13. *Id.*

14. *Edmonson v. Leesville Concrete Co.,* 500 U.S. 614 (1991)

15. *J. E. B. v. Alabama ex rel. T. B.*, 511 U.S. 127 (1994).

16. *Id.* at 129.

17. *Id.* at 141–42, *quoting Strauder v. West Virginia*, 100 U.S. 303, 308 (1880).

18. Federal Judiciary Act of 1789, 1 Stat. 73 (1789).

19. *Id.*

20. Albert Alschuler & Andrew Deiss, "A Brief History of Criminal Jury in the United States," 61 U. Chi. L. Rev. 867, 879 (1994); Brian C. Kalt, "The Exclusion of Felons from Jury Service," 53 Am. U. L. Rev. 65, 117–23 (2003).

21. Kim Taylor-Thompson, "Empty Votes in Jury Deliberations," 113 Harv. L. Rev. 1261, 1279–80 (2000); *see also* Neil Vidmar & Valerie P. Hans, *American Juries: The Verdict* (Amherst, NY: Prometheus, 2007), 71.

22. Alschuler & Deiss, "A Brief History," 61 U. Chi. L. Rev. at 884, *citing* Leon F. Litwack, *North of Slavery: The Negro in the Free States, 1780–1860* (Chicago: University of Chicago Press, 1961), 94; James Forman Jr., "Juries and Race in the Nineteenth Century," 113 Yale L.J. 895, 910–15 (2004).

23. *Jones v. Alfred H. Meyer Co.*, 392 U.S. 409, 444 (1968) (Douglas, J., concurring).

24. 18 U.S.C. § 243 (1948).

25. *Strauder v. West Virginia*, 100 U.S. 303, 308–9 (1880).

26. Alschuler & Deiss, "A Brief History," 61 U. Chi. L. Rev. at 882–901; Gretchen Ritter, "Women's Citizenship and the Problem of Legal Personhood in the United States in the 1960s and 1970s," 13 Tex. J. Women & L. 1, 14–16 (2003).

27. Jeffrey Abramson, *We the Jury: The Jury System and the Ideal of Democracy* (Cambridge: Harvard University Press, 2001), 109–10.

28. *Id.* at 109.

29. Eric M. Albritton, "Race-Conscious Grand Juror Selection: The Equal Protection Clause and Strict Scrutiny," 31 Am. J. Crim. L. 175, 204–10 (2003); Hiroshi Fukari, "Critical

Evaluations of Hispanic Participation on the Grand Jury: Key-Man Selection, Jurymandering, Language, and Representative Quotas," 5 Tex. Hisp. J. L. & Pol'y 7, 19–21 (2001).

30. Lawrence M. Friedman, "Some Notes on the Civil Jury in Historical Perspective," 48 DePaul L. Rev. 201, 215–17 (1998); Sandra Jordan, "The Criminal Jury Trial: Erosion of Jury Power," 5 Howard Scroll Soc. J. Rev. 1, 13–15 (2002).

31. Friedman, "Some Notes on the Civil Jury in Historical Perspective," 48 DePaul L. Rev. at 214.

32. *Id.*

33. *Id.*

34. Abramson, *supra* at 109.

35. Clay S. Conrad, "Scapegoating the Jury," 7 Cornell J. L. & Pub. Pol'y 7, 19–38 (1997); Timothy S. Hall, "Legal Fictions and Moral Reasoning: Capital Punishment and the Mentally Retarded Defendant After *Penry v. Johnson*," 35 Akron L. Rev. 327, n.221 (2002); Peter Arenella, "The Perils of TV Legal Punditry," 1998 U. Chi. Legal F. 25, n.16 (1998).

36. *Strauder*, 100 U.S. at 310.

37. Abramson, *supra* at 113.

38. *Id.*

39. *Fay v. New York*, 332 U.S 261 (1947).

40. *Hoyt v. Florida*, 638 U.S. 57 (1961).

41. Barbara Allen Babcock, "A Place in the Palladium: Women's Rights and Jury Service," 61 U. Cin. L. Rev. 1139, 1167 (1993); Shirley S. Abrahamson, "Justice and Juror," 20 Ga. L. Rev. 257, 267–68 (1986).

42. *Id.* at 268.

43. *Taylor v. Louisiana*, 419 U.S. 522, 532 n.13 (1975).

44. Abrahamson, "Justice and Juror," 20 Ga. L. Rev. at 269.

45. *Taylor*, 419 U.S. at 524.

46. *Id.* at 524.

47. *Id.* at 532.

48. Nancy S. Marder, "Beyond Gender: Peremptory Challenges and the Roles of the Jury," 73 Tex. L. Rev. 1041, 1096 (1995); Nancy M. Marder, "Symposium: The 50th Anniversary of *12 Angry Men*," Introduction, 82 Chi.-Kent L. Rev. 557, 572 n.89 (2007). Thanks to Professor Marder for this insight.

49. Abramson, "Justice and Juror," 20 Ga. L. Rev. at 99–100.

50. Gregory E. Mize, Paula L. Hannaford-Agor, & Nicole Waters, *The State of the States Survey of Jury Improvement Efforts*, National Center for State Courts, Executive Summary, at 5

(2010), *available at* http://www.ncsconline.org/D_Research/ cjs/state-survey.html.

51. *Taylor*, 419 U.S at 529, n.7, *quoting* H.R. Rep. No. 90-1076, at 8 (1968).

52. Douglas L. Colbert, "Liberating the Thirteenth Amendment," 30 Harv. C.R-C.L. L. Rev. 1 (1995); Andrew E. Taslitz, "Hate Crimes, Free Speech, and the Contract of Mutual Indifference," 80 B.U. L. Rev. 1283, 1379–90 (2000); William E. Forbath, "Caste, Class, and Equal Citizenship," 98 Mich. L. Rev. 1 (1999).

53. Martin Luther King Jr., "I Have a Dream" (Aug. 28, 1963), in *Words That Changed America* (Alex Barnett, ed.) (Guilford, CT: Lyons Press, 2003), 134–35.

54. Azar Nafisi, "Sivilization," The Atlantic Monthly, Nov. 2007, at 19.

55. Steven Weinberg, "Inherited Opportunity," The Atlantic Monthly, Nov. 2007, at 33–34.

56. Douglas G. Smith, "The Historical and Constitutional Contexts of Jury Reform," 25 Hofstra L. Rev. 377, 432 (1996), *citing* 4 *The Works of John Adams* 82 (Charles Francis Adams, ed.) (Boston: Little, Brown, 1851).

57. *United States v. Kandirakis*, 441 F. Supp. 2d 282, 314 (D. Mass. 2006), *quoting* Paula DiPerna, *Juries on Trial* 21 (New York: Dembner Books, 1984).

58. Phoebe A. Haddon, "Rethinking the Jury," 3 Wm. & Mary Bill of Rts. L. Rev. 29, 98–99 (1994); Vikram David Amar, "Jury Service as Political Participation Akin to Voting," 80 Cornell L. Rev. 203, 249 (1995); *see generally* Christopher E. Smith, "Imagery, Politics, and Jury Reform," 28 Akron L. Rev. 77 (1995).

59. Cornel West, "Niggarization," The Atlantic Monthly, Nov. 2007, at 20 ("Democratization is the best of the American idea—in principle and practice. The sublime notion that each and every ordinary person has a dignity that warrants his or her voice being heard in shaping the destiny of society remains a revolutionary force in the 21st century—in the face of the power of autocratic empires, plutocratic states, and xenophobic communities.").

60. *See* Roi Holt, Janvier Slick, & Amy Rayborn, "Understanding Jurors," 63 JUL Or. St. B. Bull 17, 21 (2003).

61. Philip C. Kissam, "Alexis de Tocqueville and American Constitutional Law: On Democracy, the Majority Will, Individual

Rights, Federalism, Religion, Civic Associations, and Originalist Constitutional Theory," 59 Me. L. Rev. 35, 44 (2007).

62. *United States v. Quarles*, 350 U.S. 11, 18 (1955).
63. *Peters v. Kiff*, 407 U.S. 493, 503 (1972); Tammy B. Grubb, "The Functional Effect of Eliminating Gender Bias in Jury Selection: A Critique and Analysis of *J. E. B. v. Alabama*," 48 Okla. L. Rev. 173 (1995); Marder, "Beyond Gender," 73 Tex. L. Rev. at 1041; Deborah L. Forman, "What Difference Does It Make: Gender and Jury Selection," 2 UCLA Women's L.J. 35 (1992).
64. Taylor-Thompson, "Empty Votes in Jury Deliberations," 113 Harv. L. Rev. at 1285–86; *see also* Douglas L. Colbert, "Challenging the Challenge: Thirteenth Amendment as a Prohibition Against the Racial Use of Preemptory Challenges," 76 Cornell L. Rev. 1, 208 (1990) ("Recent sociological studies also offer direct evidence that when African-American jurors are dismissed from jury duty in interracial cases, impartial jury verdicts are virtually unattainable"); Sheri Lynn Johnson, "Black Innocence and the White Jury," 83 Mich. L. Rev. 1611 (1985).
65. Vidmar & Hans, *supra* at 74–76.
66. *Id.*, *citing* Samuel Sommers, "On Racial Diversity and Group Decision Making: Identifying Multiple Effects of Racial Composition on Jury Deliberations," 90 Journal of Personality and Social Psychology 597, n.42 (2006).

Notes to Chapter 4

1. Vanue B. Lacour, "The Misunderstanding and Misuse of the Commerce Clause," 30 S. U. L. Rev. 187, n.32 (2003).
2. Mark A. Behrens, "Five Ways the Kentucky Legislature Can Improve Jury Service," 42 Brandeis L.J. 1, 5–8 (2003); Mark A. Behrens & M. Kevin Underhill, "A Call For Jury Patriotism: Why the Jury System Must Be Improved for Californians Called to Serve," 40 Cal. W. L. Rev. 135, 139–43 (2003); Kurt M. Saunders, "Race and Representation in Jury Service Selection," 36 Duq. L. Rev. 49, 70–71 (1997).
3. Bruce A. Ackerman, "The Storrs Lectures: Discovering the Constitution," 93 Yale L.J. 1013, 1020 (1984) (The *Federalist Papers* placed a high value on public activity that required sacrifice of private interests for common good in "transient and informal political associations.").
4. Cass R. Sunstein, "Beyond the Republican Revival, Symposium: The Republican Civic Tradition," 97 Yale L.J. 1539, 1547–48 (1988).

5. *Id.*

6. Gordon Wood, *The Creation of the American Republic, 1776-1787* (Chapel Hill: University of North Carolina Press, 1998) (1969), 55.

7. *Id.* at 55–56.

8. Rebecca Brown, "Accountability, Liberty, and the Constitution," 98 Colum. L. Rev. 531, 553 (1998).

9. Matthew Steilen, "Parental Rights and the State Regulation of Religious Schools," 2009 B.Y.U. Educ. & L.J. 269, 288–90 (2009); Robert W. Sheef, "Public Citizens and the Constitution: Bridging the Gap Between Popular Sovereignty and Original Intent," 69 Fordham L. Rev. 2201, 2221–22 (2001); H. Richard Ulliver & William G. Merkel, "The Second Amendment in Context: The Case of the Missing Predicate," 76 Chi.-Kent L. Rev. 403, 438–39 (2000).

10. Sunstein, "Beyond the Republican Revival," 97 Yale L.J. at 1550.

11. Wood, *supra* at 68.

12. Frank Michelman, "The Republican Civic Tradition: Law's Republic," 97 Yale L.J. 1493, 1503–4 (1988), *quoting* Hanna Pitkin, "Justice: On Relating Private and Public," 9 Pol. Theory 327, 344–45 (1981).

13. Douglas G. Smith, "An Analysis of Two Federal Structures: The Articles of Confederation and the Constitution," 34 San Diego L. Rev. 249, 270–72 (1997); Vasan Kesavan, "When Did the Articles of Confederation Cease to Be Law?" 78 Notre Dame L. Rev. 35 (2002); Paul E. McGreal, "Unconstitutional Politics," 76 Notre Dame 519, 542–48 (2001).

14. Wood, *supra* at 464.

15. *Id.*

16. *Id.*

17. Nash E. Long, "The 'Constitutional Remand': Judicial Review of Constitutionally Dubious Statutes,"14 J.L. & Pol. 667, 677 (1998).

18. *Compania General de Tabacos de Filipinas v. Collector of Internal Revenue*, 275 U.S. 87, 100 (1927) (Holmes, J., dissenting).

19. Robert Putnam, *Bowling Alone: The Collapse and Revival of American Community* (New York: Simon & Schuster, 2000).

20. *Id.* at 46.

21. *Id.* at 55–57.

22. *Id.* at 55.

23. *Id.* at 97–98, 115.

24. *Id.* at 18–19.
25. *Id.* at 19.
26. *Id.*
27. *Id.* at 288.
28. *Id.*
29. *Id.* at 288–89.
30. *Id.* at 290.
31. M. William Phelps, *Nathan Hale: The Life and Death of America's First Spy* (New York: Thomas Dunne, 2008), 192.
32. D. Graham Burnett, *A Trial by Jury* (New York: Vintage, 2001), 179.
33. Alexis de Tocqueville, *Democracy in America, Vol. 1* (Phillips Bradley, ed., 1945) (New York: Vintage, 1990), 284–85.
34. Nancy S. Marder, "Deliberations and Disclosures: A Study of Post-Verdict Interviews of Jurors," 82 Iowa L. Rev. 465, 467 (1997).

Notes to Chapter 5

1. Mary R. Rose, "Expectations of Privacy? Jurors' Views of Voir Dire Questions," 85 Judicature 10, 10–11 (2001).
2. Thomas Jefferson, Letter to L'Abbe Arnoud (July 19, 1789), 5 *The Works of Thomas Jefferson* 48 (Ford ed.) (Federal Edition) (New York: J. P Putnam's Sons, 1904) ("Were I called upon to decide whether the people had best be omitted in the Legislative or judiciary department, I would say it is better to leave them out of the legislature. The execution of the laws is more important than the making them.").
3. *See Apprendi v. New Jersey*, 530 U.S. 466, 477 (2000), *quoting* 2 J. Story, *Commentaries on the Constitution of the United States* 540–41 (Boston: Little, Brown, 4th ed., 1873); Matthew P. Harrington, "The Law-Finding Function of the American Jury," 1999 Wis. L. Rev. 377, 396 (1999).
4. *United States ex rel. Toth v. Quarles*, 350 U.S. 11, 18–19 (1955).
5. James Madison, 1 Annals of Cong. 454 (J. Gales ed., 1789).
6. James Madison, *The Writings of James Madison, Vol. 6* (Gaillard Hunt, ed., 1906) (1792) (New York: J. P Putnam's Sons), 83.
7. Laura I. Appleman, "The Lost Meaning of the Jury Trial Right," 84 Ind. L.J. 397, 427–28 (2009).
8. Stephan Landsman, "The Civil Jury in America: Scenes from an Unappreciated History," 44 Hastings L.J. 579, 598 (1993).
9. *Id.* at 598; Edith G. Henderson, "The Background of the Seventh Amendment," 80 Harv. L. Rev. 289, 292 (1966); Douglas

G. Smith, "Structural and Functional Aspects of the Jury: Comparative Analysis and Proposals for Reform," 48 Ala. L. Rev. 441, 471, n.89 (1997); Pamela J. Stevens, "Controlling the Civil Jury: Towards a Functional Model of Justification," 76 Ky. L.J. 81, 86–87 (1987).

10. Appleman, "The Lost Meaning," 84 Ind. L.J. at 427–28; Landsman, "The Civil Jury in America," 44 Hastings L. J. at 598; Stevens, "Controlling the Civil Jury," 76 Ky. L.J. at 87.

11. Appleman, "The Lost Meaning," 84 Ind. L.J. at 427–28; Vikram David Amar, "Jury Service as Political Participation Akin to Voting," 80 Cornell L. Rev. 203, 218–19 (1995); Smith, "Structural and Functional Aspects of the Jury," 48 Ala. L. Rev. at n.109.

12. Landsman, "The Civil Jury in America," 44 Hastings L.J. at 600.

13. *Id.* at 599.

14. *Id.* at 600.

15. *Id.* at 581.

16. Patrick Henry, Address to the Virginia Convention (March 23, 1775), in *The World's Best Orations From the Earliest Period to the Present Time, Vol. 7* (David J. Brewer, ed., 1901) (Akron, OH: Werner Co., 1899), 2477.

17. George Washington, Farewell Address (Sept. 19, 1796), in *Words That Changed America* (Alex Barnett, ed.) (Guilford, CT: Lyons Press, 2003).

18. Forrest McDonald, *Novus Ordo Seclorum: The Intellectual Origins of the Constitution* (Lawrence: University of Kansas Press 1985), 10.

19. *See, for example, Gregory v. City of Chicago*, 394 U.S. 111, 113 (1969); *Terminello v. City of Chicago*, 377 U.S. 1, 3 (1949); *Stromberg v. California*, 283 U.S. 359, 363–64 (1931); *Gitlow v. New York*, 268 U.S. 652, 672 (1925) (Holmes, J., dissenting).

20. *See, for example, United States v. Ballard*, 322 U.S. 78, 79 (1944).

21. Edmund A. Opitz, "The American Way in Economics," The Freeman, Oct. 1964, at 46.

22. *Marbury v. Madison*, 5 U.S. (1 Cranch) 137, 174–75 (1803).

23. Akhil Reed Amar, "Textualism and the Bill of Rights," 66 Geo. Wash. L. Rev. 1143, 1145 (1998).

24. The above insight comes from the work of Akhil Reed Amar, *id.* at 1144.

25. Akhil Reed Amar, "The Bill of Rights as a Constitution," 100 Yale L.J. 1131, 1152 (1991).

26. *Id.* at 1174.
27. *West Virginia Board of Education v. Barnette*, 319 U.S. 624, 638 (1943).
28. Thomas Paine, *The American Crisis No. IV*, in *The Writings of Thomas Paine* (Moncure D. Conway, ed., 1906) (1894) (New York: J. P. Putnam's Sons), 229.
29. Laurence H. Tribe, "Trial by Mathematics: Precision and Ritual in the Legal Process," 84 Harv. L. Rev. 1329, 1392 (1971).
30. *Blakely v. Washington*, 542 U.S. 296, 313–14 (2004) (internal citations and quotation marks omitted).
31. Rachel E. Barkow, "Recharging the Jury: The Criminal Jury's Constitutional Role in an Era of Mandatory Sentencing," 152 U. Pa. L. Rev. 33, 33 (2003), *citing* William Blackstone, Commentaries; *Jones v. United States*, 526 U.S. 227, 246 (1999).
32. Patrick E. Higginbotham, "Continuing the Dialogue: Civil Juries and the Allocation of Judicial Power," 56 Tex. L. Rev. 47, 58–60 (1977).
33. *Id.* at 59–60.
34. The Declaration of Independence, para. 2 (U.S. 1776).
35. Raoul Berger, "Liberty and the Constitution," 29 Ga. L. Rev. 585, 586–87 (1995), *quoting The Papers of Alexander Hamilton, Vol. IV* (H. Syrett et al., eds., 1962) (New York: Columbia University Press, 1962), 35.
36. *Id.* at 587, *quoting* Alfred Avins, *The Reconstruction Amendments' Debates* (Richmond: Virginia Commission on Constitutional Government, 1967), 529.
37. *Meyer v. Nebraska*, 262 U.S. 390, 399 (1923).
38. Nancy S. Marder, "Bringing Jury Instructions into the Twenty-First Century," 81 Notre Dame L. Rev. 449, 454–58 (2006); Peter Tiersma, "The Rocky Road to Legal Reform: Improving the Language of Jury Instructions," 6 Brook. L. Rev. 1081, 1084–98 (2001); Bethany K. Dumas, "Jury Trials: Lay Jurors, Pattern Instructions, and Comprehension Issues," 67 Tenn. L. Rev. 701, 702–5 (2000).
39. Marder, "Bringing Jury Instructions into the Twenty-First Century," 81 Notre Dame L. Rev. at 475–82; Dumas, "Lay Jurors, Pattern Instructions, and Comprehension Issues," 67 Tenn. L. Rev. at 739–41.
40. Stephen Breyer, *Active Liberty: Interpreting Our Democratic Constitution* (New York: Alfred A. Knopf, 2005), 3 (emphasis added).
41. *Id.* at 15–16.
42. *Id.*

Notes to Chapter 6

1. Christopher N. May, "What Do We Do Now? Helping Juries Apply the Instructions," 28 Loy. L.A. L. Rev. 869, 877 (1995). The American Judicature Society has developed a short pamphlet to address the "how to deliberate" question for judges. *See* "Behind Closed Doors: A Guide for Jury Deliberation" (American Judicature Society 1999).

2. Neil Vidmar & Valerie P. Hans, *American Juries: The Verdict* (Amherst, NY: Prometheus, 2007), at 143–44.

3. *Id.* at 143.

4. *Id.*

5. *Id.*

6. Dennis J. Devine et al., "Jury Decision Making: 45 Years of Empirical Research on Deliberating Groups," 7 Psychol. Pub. Pol'y & L. 622, 701 (2001); Michael J. Saks, "What Do Jury Experiments Tell Us About How Juries (Should) Make Decisions?" 6 S. Cal. Interdisc. L.J. 1, 40 (1997); Shari Seidman Diamond et al., "Revisiting the Unanimity Requirement: The Behavior of the Non-unanimous Civil Jury," 100 Nw. U. L. Rev. 201, 225–26 (2006).

7. Leonard Levy, *Origins of the Bill of Rights* (New Haven: Yale University Press, 2001), 211; *see also* Douglas G. Smith, "The Historical and Constitutional Contexts of Jury Reform," 25 Hofstra L. Rev. 377, 396 (1996).

8. Levy, *supra* at 215.

9. *Duncan v. Louisiana*, 391 U.S. 145, 151–52, *quoting* 4 William Blackstone Commentaries at 349–50: "[T]he truth of every accusation, whether preferred in the shape of indictment, information, or appeal, should afterwards be confirmed by the unanimous suffrage of twelve of his equals and neighbours, indifferently chosen and superior to all suspicion."

10. Michael J. Saks, "The Smaller the Jury, the Greater the Unpredictability," 79 Judicature 263, 263 (1996).

11. Jeffrey Abramson, *We the Jury: The Jury System and the Ideal of Democracy* (Cambridge: Harvard University Press, 2001), 179, *quoting Thompson v. Utah*, 170 U.S. 343, 353 (1898).

12. *Williams v. Florida*, 399 U.S. 78, 87 (1970); *Colgrove v. Battin*, 413 U.S. 149 (1973).

13. Saks, "The Smaller the Jury," 79 Judicature at 263.

14. *Williams v. Florida*, 399 U.S. 78, 87–90 (1970).

15. *See* American Bar Association, *Principles for Juries and Jury Trials*, "Principle 3, Juries Should Have 12 Members" (August

2005), 15; Saks, "The Smaller the Jury," 79 Judicature at 263; Hans Zeisel, "And Then There Were None: The Diminution of the Federal Jury," 38 U. Chi. L. Rev. 710 (1971).

16. Saks, "The Smaller the Jury," 79 Judicature at 263.

17. *Id.* at 265.

18. *Id.* at 264.

19. *Id.* at 265.

20. *Ballew v. Georgia*, 435 U.S. 223, 230 (1978).

21. Stephan Landsman, "Appellate Courts and Civil Juries," 70 U. Cin. L. Rev. 873, 906 (2002); Douglas G. Smith, "Structural and Functional Aspects of the Jury: Comparative Analysis and Proposals for Reform," 48 Ala. L. Rev. at 517–22; Christopher E. Smith, "Imagery, Politics, and Jury Reform," 28 Akron L. Rev. 77, 90–91 (1995).

22. 435 U.S. at 230, *citing* Michael J. Saks, *Jury Verdicts* (Lexington, Mass.: Lexington Books, 1977); *see also* A. W. Bogue & T. G. Fritz, "The Six-Man Jury," 17 S.D. L. Rev. 285 (1972); James H. Davis et al., "The Decision Processes of 6- and 12-Person Mock Juries Assigned Unanimous and Two-Thirds Majority Rules," 32 J. of Personality & Soc. Psych. 1 (1975); Sheri Seidman Diamond, "A Jury Experiment Reanalyzed," 7 U. Mich. J.L. Reform 520 (1974); Herbert Friedman, "Trial by Jury: Criteria for Convictions, Jury Size, and Type I and Type II Errors," 26 Am. Statistician 21 (1972); Richard O. Lempert, "Uncovering 'Nondiscernible' Differences: Empirical Research and the Jury-Size Cases," 73 Mich. L. Rev. 643 (1975); William R. Pabst, "Statistical Studies of the Costs of Six-Man Versus Twelve-Man Juries," 14 Wm. & Mary L. Rev. 326 (1972); Michael J. Saks, "Ignorance of Science Is No Excuse," 10 Trial, Nov./Dec. 1974, at 18; Hans Zeisel, "Twelve Is Just," 10 Trial, Nov./Dec. 1974, at 13; Hans Zeisel, "The Waning of the American Jury," 58 A.B.A. J. 367 (1972); Hans Zeisel & Sheri Seidman Diamond, "Convincing Empirical Evidence on the Six Member Jury," 41 U. Chi. L. Rev. 281 (1974); David F. Walbert, "The Effect of Jury Size on the Probability of Conviction: An Evaluation of *Williams v. Florida*," 22 Case W. Res. L. Rev. 529 (1971); "Six-Member and Twelve-Member Juries: An Empirical Study of Trial Results," 6 U. Mich. J. L. Reform 671 (1973).

23. U.S. Dept. of Justice, *State Court Organization, 2004*, at 233–336, *available at* http://bjs.ojp.usdoj.gov/content/pub/pdf/sco04.pdf.

24. Fed. R. Civ. P. 48(a)–(b).

25. Nancy S. Marder, "Deliberations and Disclosures: A Study of Post-Verdict Interviews of Jurors," 82 Iowa L. Rev. 465, 468 (1997).

26. *Ballew v. Georgia*, 435 U.S. 223, 230 (1978), *citing Williams v. Florida*, 399 U.S. 78, 100 (1970).

27. Deliberation, of course, predates the Constitution. All thirteen colonies had local town councils and public assemblies, and the tradition of jury trials dates back to the Magna Carta. The Roman Senate, the Greek demos, and prerevolutionary American experience all shaped the principles of America's political development. Deliberation is thus not uniquely American, but we have made it ours through our governing structure and daily practice.

28. Bruce Ackerman & Neal Katyal, "Our Unconventional Founding," 62 U. Chi. L. Rev. 475, 481 (1995).

29. Henry Paul Monaghan, "We the People(s), Original Understanding, and Constitutional Amendment," 96 Colum. L. Rev. 121, 139–46 (1996).

30. *Id.* at 139–43.

31. Richard B. Bernstein, "The Sleeper Wakes: The History and Legacy of the Twenty-Seventh Amendment," 61 Fordham L. Rev. 497 (1992); Calvin H. Johnson, "Homage to Clio: The Historical Continuity from the Articles of Confederation into the Constitution," 20 Const. Commentary 463 (2003/4); Price Marshall, "A Careless Written Letter: Situating Amendments to the Federal Constitution," 51 Ark. L. Rev. 95 (1998).

32. Federalist Paper No. 1 (Alexander Hamilton).

33. *Id.*

34. Peter Irons, *A People's History of the Supreme Court* (New York: Penguin, 1999), 60.

35. John Adams, "Letter from the Earl of Caledon to William Pym," January 27, 1776, *The Works of John Adams, Second President of the United States: With a Life of the Author, Notes, and Illustrations* (Charles Francis Adams, ed.) (Boston: Little, Brown, 1856).

36. The idea of the Senate as the deliberative body comes in part from Edmund Burke's famous observation of the Parliament of England: "Parliament is not a *congress* of ambassadors from different and hostile interests . . . [it is] a *deliberative* assembly of *one* nation, with *one* interest, that of the whole." Jack N. Rakove, "From the Old Congress to the New," in *The American Congress: The Building of Democracy* (Julian E. Zelizer,

ed.) (New York: Houghton Mifflin, 2004), 6, *quoting* Edmund Burke, Speech to the Electors of Bristol (Nov. 3 1774).

37. The Senate record is held by the late Senator Strom Thurmond, who filibustered the 1957 Civil Rights Act by speaking for twenty-four hours and eighteen minutes. "Thurmond Holds Senate Record for Filibustering," Associated Press, June 27, 2003, *available at* http://www.foxnews.com/story/0,2933,90552,00.html.

38. Charles W. Johnson IV, "The Doctrine of Official Immunity: An Unnecessary Intrusion into Speech or Debate Clause," 43 Cath. U. L. Rev. 535, 539, n.27 (1994), recognizing that the English Bill of Rights states, "The freedom of speech and debates, or proceedings in parliament, ought not to be impeached or questioned in any court or place out of parliament." 1 W. & M., Sess. 2, ch. 2 (1689).

39. Richard K. Neumann Jr., "The Revival of Impeachment as a Partisan Political Weapon," 34 Hastings Const. L.Q. 161, 217–27 (2007); Keith A. Whittington, "Bill Clinton Was No Andrew Johnson: Comparing Two Impeachments," 2 U. Pa. J. Const. L. 422, 442–50 (2000); Jonathan Turley, "Senate Trials and Factional Disputes: Impeachment as a Madisonian Device," 49 Duke L.J. 1, 84–92 (1999).

40. Alison Mitchel, "The President's Acquittal: The Overview; Clinton Acquitted Decisively: No Majority for Either Charge," New York Times (Feb. 13, 1999).

41. Bruce Ackerman, *We the People, Volume 1: Foundations* (Cambridge: Harvard University Press, 1991), 15.

42. Alisa Smith & Michael Saks, "The Case for Overturning *Williams v. Florida* and the Six-Person Jury: History, Law, and Empirical Evidence," 60 Fla. L. Rev. 441, 446 (2008); Michael J. Saks & Mollie Weighner Marti, "A Meta-analysis of the Effects of Jury Size," 21 Law & Hum. Behav. 451 (1997); Vicki L. Smith, "How Jurors Make Decisions: The Value of Trial Innovations," in *Jury Trial Innovations* (G. Thomas Munsterman et al., eds.) (Williamsburg, VA: National Center for State Courts, 1997), 5.

43. Devine et al., "Jury Decision Making," 7 Psychol. Pub. Pol'y & L at 669; Valerie P. Hans, "The Power of Twelve: The Impact of Jury Size and Unanimity on Civil Jury Decision Making," 4 Del. L. Rev. 2, 23 (2001); Lempert, "Uncovering 'Nondiscernible' Differences," 73 Mich. L. Rev. at 645; Reid Hastie et al., *Inside the Jury* (Cambridge: Harvard University Press, 1983), 45–58.

44. William L. Dwyer, *In the Hands of the People: The Trial Jury's Origins, Triumphs, Troubles, and Future in American Democracy* (New York: Thomas Dunne, St. Martin's Press, 2002), 152.

45. Vidmar & Hans, *supra* at 144.

46. *See* note 42.

47. *Ballew v. Georgia*, 435 U.S. 223, 230 (1978).

48. *See* American Bar Association, *supra*, "Principle 4, Juries Should Be Unanimous," at 21; Devine et al., "Jury Decision Making," 7 Psychol. Pub. Pol'y & L at 669.

49. Hastie, *supra* at 45–58; Hans, "The Power of Twelve," 4 Del. L. Rev. at 23; Lempert, "Uncovering 'Nondiscernible' Differences," 73 Mich. L. Rev. at 645. In studies on nonunanimous verdicts, less information was produced; and in 70 percent of cases in which a majority developed, the jury did not reach a consensus. *See* Kim Taylor-Thompson, "Empty Votes in Jury Deliberations," 113 Harv. L. Rev. 1261, 1273 (2000).

50. Marder, "Deliberations and Disclosures," 82 Iowa L. Rev. at 472.

51. *Id.*

52. Douglas H. Cook, "How I Spent My Sabbatical, or What Happens When a Torts Professor Is a Juror in a Negligence Case," 14 Rev. Litig. 219, 234 (1994).

53. *See* Roi Holt, Janvier Slick, & Amy Rayborn, "Understanding Jurors," 63 JUL Or. St. B. Bull 17 (2003) (interviewing jurors who said, "I was tied up in knots, deciding this man's fate," and "It was traumatic to make decision regarding the fate of a person.").

54. Benjamin Franklin, *On the Federal Constitution* (1787), in *The World's Famous Orations, Vol. VIII* (William Jennings Bryan, ed.) (New York: Funk and Wagnalls, 1906), 54.

55. The response was, "The opinions I have had of its errors, I sacrifice to the public good." *Id.* at 54.

Notes to Chapter 7

1. Reginald Rose, *Twelve Angry Men*, in *Film Scripts Two* (George P. Garrett, O. B. Hardison, & Jane R. Gelfman, eds.) (New York: Irvington, 1989) (1972), 156, 189 (screenplay version of the film *12 Angry Men*, Orion-Nova Productions, 1957).

2. *Id.* at 178.

3. "Symposium: The 50th Anniversary of *12 Angry Men*," 82 Chi.-Kent L. Rev. 551 (2007); Nancy S. Marder, "Symposium: The 50th Anniversary of *12 Angry Men*," Introduction, 82 Chi-Kent

L. Rev. 557, 557–60 (2007); Valerie P. Hans, "Deliberation and Dissent: *12 Angry Men* Versus the Reality of Juries," 82 Chi.-Kent L. Rev. 779, 779–82 (2007); Judith S. Kaye, "Why Every Chief Judge Should See *12 Angry Men*," 82 Chi.-Kent L. Rev. 627 (2007).

4. Hans, "Deliberation and Dissent," 82 Chi.-Kent L. Rev at 582–89; Barbara Allen Babcock & Ticien Marie Sassoubre, "Deliberation in *12 Angry Men*," 82 Chi.-Kent L. Rev. 633 (2007); Stephan Landsman, "Mad About *12 Angry Men*," 82 Chi-Kent. L. Rev. 749 (2007).

5. *See, for example*, 9th Cir. Pattern Crim. Jury Instructions § 8.03 (Unanimous Verdict).

6. Jeffrey Abramson, *We the Jury: The Jury System and the Ideal of Democracy* (Cambridge: Harvard University Press, 2001), at 179.

7. *Id.*; Stephan Landsman, "The Civil Jury in America: Scenes from an Unappreciated History," 44 Hastings L.J. 579, 586 (1993); Douglas G. Smith, "The Historical and Constitutional Contexts of Jury Reform," 25 Hofstra L. Rev. 377, 397 (1996).

8. *Thompson v. Utah*, 170 U.S. 343, 353 (1898); *Andres v. United States*, 333 U.S. 740, 748–49 (1948); *Patton v. United States*, 281 U.S. 276, 288–90 (1930); *Hawaii v. Mankichi*, 190 U.S. 197, 211–12 (1903); *Maxwell v. Dow*, 176 U.S. 581, 586 (1900); Abramson, *supra* at 179; Fed. R. Crim. P. 31(2) (2004).

9. Abramson, *supra* at 180.

10. *Id.*

11. Pattern Federal Jury Instructions for the Seventh Circuit Court of Appeals, available http://www.ca7.uscourts.gov/pjury.pdf (emphasis added).

12. William L. Dwyer, *In the Hands of the People: The Trial Jury's Origins, Triumphs, Troubles, and Future in American Democracy* (New York: Thomas Dunne, St. Martin's Press, 2002), 56.

13. Maj. Bradley J. Huestis, "Calling for Candor from the Bench and Bar," 173 Mil. L. Rev. 68, 73–74 (2002); Michael I. Meyerson, "The Neglected History of the Prior Restraint Doctrine: Rediscovering the Link Between the First Amendment and the Separation of Powers," 34 Ind. L. Rev. 295, 306–8 (2001); M. Kristine Creagan, "Jury Nullification: Assessing Recent Legal Developments," 43 Case W. Res. L. Rev. 1101, 1105–6 (1993).

14. George C. Thomas III & Mark Greenbaum, "Justice Story Cuts the Gordian Knot of Hung Jury Instructions," 15 Wm.

& Mary L. Rev. 893, 898–90 (2007); Sanjeev Anand, "The Origins, Early History, and Evolution of the English Criminal Trial Jury," 43 Alberta L. Rev. 407, 429–30 (2005); Nancy S. Marder, "The Myth of Nullifying the Jury," 93 Nw. U. L. Rev. 877, n.336 (1999).

15. Dwyer, *supra* at 52.

16. *Id*. at 54.

17. Paul Butler, "Racially Based Jury Nullification: Black Power in the Criminal Justice System," 105 Yale L.J. 677, 701–2 (1995); Stephanie Domitrovich, "Jury Source Lists and the Community's Need to Achieve Racial Balance on the Jury," 33 Duq. L. Rev. 39, 47–48 (1994).

18. Dwyer, *supra* at 54.

19. *Id*.

20. Joe Jamail, "The Presentation of an Ethical Jury Trial," 47 S. Tex. L. Rev. 357, 363–64 (2005).

21. Dwyer, *supra* at 55–56; Jamail, "Presentation," 47 S. Tex. L. Rev. at 363–64.

22. Dwyer, *supra* at 55; Jamail, "Presentation," 47 S. Tex. L. Rev. at 363–64.

23. Jamail, "Presentation," 47 S. Tex. L. Rev. at 363–64.

24. Dwyer, *supra* at 55–56.

25. *Id*. at 57.

26. *Id*.

27. John D. Jackson, "Making Juries Accountable," 50 Am. J. Comp. L. 477, 491–94 (2002); Huestis, "Calling for Candor," 173 Mil. L. Rev. at 75–94; Butler, *supra* at 701–3.

28. Dwyer, *supra* at 50; *see also* R. J. Farley, "Instructions to Juries—Their Role in the Judicial Process," 42 Yale L.J. 194, 196–97 (1932).

29. *Sparf v. United States*, 156 U.S. 51, 90–91 (1895); David A. Pepper, "Nullifying History: Modern-Day Misuse of the Right to Decide the Law," 50 Case W. Res. L. Rev. 599, 612–13 (2000); Butler, "Racially Based Jury Nullification," 105 Yale L.J. at 701–2.

30. Meyerson, "The Neglected History of the Prior Restraint Doctrine," 34 Ind. L. Rev. at 306.

31. *Locke v. Davis*, 540 U.S. 712 (2004); *Lee v. Weisman*, 505 U.S. 577, 591–92 (1992); *Wallace v. Jaffree*, 472 U.S. 38, 53–55 (1985).

32. Akhil Reed Amar, *The Bill of Rights: Creation and Reconstruction* (New Haven: Yale University Press, 1998), at 23–24.

33. Garry Wills, *Head and Heart: American Christianities* (New York: Penguin, 2007), 74: "All of the most influential early colonizers from England were products of the Reformation (Catholics and Jews were a minority factor)."

34. Jon Meacham, *American Gospel: God, the Founding Fathers, and the Making of a Nation* (New York: Random House, 2006), 52.

35. Wills, *supra* at 5–6.

36. Martha Nussbaum, "Living Together: The Roots of Respect," 2008 U. Ill. L. Rev. 1623 (2008); Timothy L. Hall, "Roger Williams and the Foundations of Religious Liberty," 71 B.U. L. Rev. 455 (1991); Michael W. McConnell, "The Origins and Historical Understanding of the Free Exercise of Religion," 103 Harv. L. Rev. 1409, 1424–27 (1990).

37. James Madison, "To the Honorable the General Assembly of the Commonwealth of Virginia: A Memorial and a Remonstrance" (June 20, 1785), *cited by Everson v. Bd. of Educ.*, 330 U.S. 1, 64 (1947).

38. *Cantwell v. Connecticut*, 310 U.S. 296, 306 (1940).

39. *Lynch v. Donnelly*, 465 U.S. 668, 687 (1984) (O'Connor, J., concurring).

40. *Lee v. Weisman*, 505 U.S. 577, 606 (1992), *quoting* 1 Annals of Cong. 757 (1789).

41. *Everson v. Board of Education*, 330 U.S. 1, 15–16 (1947).

42. Meacham, *supra* at 33.

43. *Id.* at 69.

44. *Id.* (emphasis added).

45. *Id.*

46. Roger A. Fairfax Jr., "Grand Jury Discretion and Constitutional Design," 93 Cornell L. Rev. 703, 722 (2008); Pepper, "Nullifying History," 50 Case W. Res. L. Rev. at 622–26; Michael T. Gibson, "The Supreme Court and Freedom of Expression from 1791 to 1917," 55 Fordham L. Rev. 263, n.51 (1986).

47. Frederick Schauer, "The Role of the People in First Amendment Theory," 74 Cal. L. Rev. 761, 765 (1986).

48. J. Wilson Parker, "Free Expression and the Function of the Jury," 65 B.U. L. Rev. 483, 504–8 (1985).

49. Amar, *supra* at 24; Schauer, "The Role of the People in First Amendment Theory," 74 Cal. L. Rev. at 765; Akhil Reed Amar, "The Bill of Rights as a Constitution," 100 Yale L.J. 1131, 1150 (1991).

50. *Abrams v. United States*, 250 U.S. 616, 630 (1919) (Holmes, J., dissenting).

51. Akhil Reed Amar, "2000 Daniel J. Meador Lecture: Hugo Black and the Hall of Fame" (Oct. 23, 2000), 53 Ala. L. Rev. 1221 1238–39 (2000); Patricia M. Stembridge, "Adjusting Absolutism: First Amendment Protection for the Fringe," 80 B.U. L. Rev. 907, 917–18 (2000); Steven J. Heyman, "Righting the Balance: An Inquiry into the Foundations and Limits of Freedom of Expression," 78 B.U. L. Rev. 1275, 1347–49 (1998).

52. *New York Times v. Sullivan*, 376 U.S. 254, 270 (1964).

53. *Whitney v. California*, 274 U.S. 357, 375 (1927).

54. William E. Lee, "Lonely Pamphleteers, Little People, and the Supreme Court: The Doctrine of Time, Place, and Manner Regulations of Expression," 54 Geo. Wash. L. Rev. 757 (1986); Robert H. Whorf, "The Dangerous Intersection at 'Prior Expression' and 'Time, Place, Manner': A Comment on *Thomas v. Chicago Park District*," 3 Barry L. Rev. 1, 5–8 (2002); Tim Cramm, "The Designated Non-public Forum: Remedying the Forbes Mistake," 67 Alb. L. Rev. 89, 145–47 (2003).

55. Geoffrey Stone, *Perilous Times: Free Speech in Wartime from the Sedition Act of 1789 to the War on Terrorism* (New York: Norton, 2004), 7.

56. Vincent Martin Bonventre, "The Fall of Free Exercise: From No Law to Compelling Interests to Any Law Otherwise Valid," 70 Alb. L. Rev. 1399, 1408–10 (2007); Patrick J. Flynn, "Writing Their Faith into the Laws of the Land: Jehovah's Witness's and the Supreme Court's Battle for the Meaning of the Free Exercise Clause, 1939–1945," 1 Tex. J. C.L. & C.R. 1 (2004); David E. Steinberg, "Rejecting the Case Against the Free Exercise Exemption: A Critical Assessment," 75 B.U. L. Rev. 241, 260–63 (1995).

57. Abramson, *supra* n.26, at 197.

58. *Id*. at 198.

59. Kim Taylor-Thompson, "Empty Votes in Jury Deliberations," 113 Harv. L. Rev. 1261, 1317 (2000), *citing* Michael J. Saks, "What Do Jury Experiments Tell Us About How Juries (Should) Make Decisions?" 6 S. Cal. Indisc. L.J. 1, 41 (1997).

60. William Glaberson, "For Judges, Lawyers, and Fellow Jurors, the Challenges of Dealing with a Holdout," New York Times (Nov. 19, 2010) (describing one juror's reaction in the prosecution of Tyco executives).

61. Dwyer, *supra* at 79–80.

62. *Id.* at 80.

63. *Id.*

64. *Id.* at 80–81.

65. Hans Zeisel, "And Then There Were None: The Diminution of the Federal Jury," 38 U. Chi. L. Rev. 711, 719 n.42 (1971), *quoted in* Abramson, *supra* at 200.

66. Dwyer, *supra* at 81.

67. Meacham, *supra* at 18.

68. *Id.* at 25–27.

69. *Id.* at 23.

Notes to Chapter 8

1. William J. Bowers et al., "Too Young for the Death Penalty: An Empirical Examination of Community Conscience and the Juvenile Death Penalty from the Perspective of Capital Jurors," 84 B.U. L. Rev. 609, 627–33 (2004); James Joseph Duane, "What Message Are We Sending to Criminal Jurors When We Ask Them to 'Send a Message' with Their Verdict?" 22 Am. J. Crim. L. 565, 590–97 (1995); *Jones v. United States,* 527 U.S. 373, 382 (1999); *Witherspoon v. Illinois,* 391 U.S. 510, 519 (1968) ("[A] jury that must choose between life imprisonment and capital punishment can do little more—and must do nothing less—than express the conscience of the community on the ultimate question of life or death").

2. Nancy S. Marder, "Deliberations and Disclosures: A Study of Post-verdict Interviews of Jurors," 82 Iowa L. Rev. 465, 484–85 (1997).

3. *Texaco Inc. v. Pennzoil Co.,* 729 S.W. 2d 768 (1987), cert dismissed 485 U.S. 994 (1988); *see also* J. S. Bainbridge Jr., "Texaco's Last Stand," 73 A.B.A. J. 110 (1987); Robert M. Lloyd, "*Pennzoil v. Texaco,* Twenty Years After: Lessons for Business Lawyers," 6 Transactions 321, 321–51 (2005); Stephan Landsman, "The Civil Jury in America," 62 Law & Contemp. Probs. 285, 287 (1999).

4. Landsman, "The Civil Jury in America," 62 Law & Contemp. Probs., at 287; Alexander Tabarrok & Eric Helland, "Court Politics: The Political Economy of Tort Awards," 42 J. L. & Econ. 157, 161 (1999); Doug Rendelman, "A Cap on the Defendant's Appeal Bond? Punitive Damages Tort Reform," 39 Akron L. Rev. 1089, 1106–7 (2006).

5. *Victor v. Nebraska,* 511 U.S. 1, 5 (1994); Duane, "What Message Are We Sending," 22 Am. J. Crim. L. at 665–66; Jessica N. Cohen, "The Reasonable Doubt Jury Instruction: Giving

Meaning to a Critical Concept," 22 Am. J. Crim. L. 677, 688–701 (1995); Thomas V. Mulrine, "Reasonable Doubt: How in the World Is It Defined?" 12 Am. U. J. Int'l. L. Rev. 195 (1997).

6. *In re Winship*, 397 U.S. 358, 364 (1970); *Apprendi v. New Jersey*, 530 U.S. 466, 483–84 (2000).

7. *In re Winship*, 397 U.S. at 364.

8. *Id.*

9. Rachel E. Barkow, "Recharging the Jury: The Criminal Jury's Constitutional Role in an Era of Mandatory Sentencing," 152 U. Pa. L. Rev. 33, 64–65 (2003).

10. *Blakely v. Washington*, 542 U.S. 296, 305–6 (2004).

11. Akhil Reed Amar, "Double Jeopardy Law Made Simple," 106 Yale L.J. 1807, 1846 (1997).

12. *Jones v. United States*, 526 U.S. 227, 247 (1999), *citing* Leonard Levy, *Freedom of Speech and Press in Early American History* (New York: Harper, 1963), 133; Albert Alschuler & Andrew Deiss, "A Brief History of Criminal Jury in the United States," 61 U. Chi. L. Rev. 867, 871–74 (1994).

13. William R. Glendon, "The Trial of John Peter Zenger," 68 N.Y. St. B. J. 48, 49 (1996).

14. James G. Wilson, "The Role of Public Opinion in Constitutional Interpretation," 1993 B.Y.U. L. Rev. 1037, 1051–53 (1993); Fredrick Shauer, "The Role of the People in First Amendment Theory," 74 Cal. L. Rev. 761, 761–64 (1986); J. Wilson Parker, "Free Expression and the Function of the Jury," 65 B.U. L. Rev. 483, 502–3 (1985); *McIntyre v. Ohio Elections Comm'n*, 514 U.S. 334, 361 (1995).

15. Glendon, "The Trial of John Peter Zenger," 68 Dec. N.Y. St. B. J. at 50.

16. *Id.* at 48.

17. *Id.* at 50.

18. *Id.*

19. *Id.*

20. Alschuler & Deiss, "A Brief History," 61 U. Chi. L. Rev. at 873–74; Lawrence W. Crispo et al., "Jury Nullification: Law Versus Anarchy," 31 Loy. L.A. L. Rev. 1, 7–8 (1997); Welsh S. White, "Fact-Finding and the Death Penalty: The Scope of a Capital Defendant's Right to a Jury Trial," 65 Notre Dame L. Rev. 1, n.97 (1989).

21. Glendon, "The Trial of John Peter Zenger," 68 Dec. N.Y. St. B. J. at 50.

22. *Id.*

23. *Id.* at 51.
24. *Id.*
25. *Id.* at 52.
26. *Id.*
27. *Jones v. United States*, 526 U.S. 227, 247 (1999), citing Leonard Levy, *Legacy of Suppression: Freedom of Speech and Press in Early American History* (New York: Harper, 1963), 133; Alschuler & Deiss, "A Brief History," 61 U. Chi. L. Rev. at 871; *Cohen v. Hurley*, 366 U.S. 81, 140 (1961).
28. *Duncan v. Louisiana*, 391 U.S. 145, 155–56 (1968); *see also Singer v. United States*, 380 U.S. 24, 31 (1965); *United States v. Booker*, 543 U.S. 220, 238–39 (2005).
29. Alschuler & Deiss, "A Brief History," 61 U. Chi. L. Rev. at 905.
30. Stanton D. Krauss, "An Inquiry into the Right of Criminal Juries to Determine the Law in Colonial America," 89 J. Crim. L. & Criminology 111, 116 (1998).
31. David A. Pepper, "Nullifying History: The Modern-Day Misuse of the Right to Decide the Law," 50 Case W. Res. L. Rev. 599 (2000); Lawrence W. Crispo et al., "Jury Nullification: Law Versus Anarchy," 31 Loy. L.A. L. Rev. 1 (1997); Paul Butler, "Racially Based Jury Nullification: Black Power in the Criminal Justice System," 105 Yale L.J. 677 (1995); M. Kristine Creagan, "Jury Nullification: Assessing Recent Legal Developments," 43 Case W. Res. L. Rev. 1101 (1993); *United States v. Dougherty*, 473 F. 2d 1113, 1130–37 (D.C. Cir. 1972).
32. *U.S. Term Limits Inc. v. Thornton*, 514 U.S. 779, 838–39 (1995) (Kennedy, J., concurring).
33. The list in the text comes from the United States Constitution. However, a wonderful summary can be found at "Constitutional Topic: Checks and Balances," http://usconstitution.net/consttop_cnb.html. I used this website to organize the material in the book.
34. *Youngstown Sheet & Tube Co. v. Sawyer*, 343 U.S. 579, 635 (1952) (Jackson, J., concurring).
35. Shari Seidman Diamond & Neil Vidmar, "Jury Room Ruminations on Forbidden Topics," 87 Va. L. Rev. 1857, 1860–61 (2001).
36. James E. Kelly, "Addressing Juror Stress: A Trial Judge's Perspective," 43 Drake L. Rev. 97, 97 (1994) ("The cases that do go to trial are the ones in which either the stakes are too high for compromise, or the principles involved seem too important to be negotiated.").

37. *Blakely v. Washington*, 542 U.S. at 306.

38. Barkow, "Recharging the Jury," 152 U. Pa. L. Rev. at 122.

39. *Smith v. Texas*, 311 U.S. 128, 130 (1948).

40. Marder, "Deliberations and Disclosures," 82 Iowa L. Rev. at 468.

41. Vikram David Amar, "Jury Service as Political Participation," 80 Cornell L. Rev. at 218.

42. Douglas H. Cook, "How I Spent My Sabbatical, or What Happens When a Torts Professor Is a Juror in a Negligence Case," 14 Rev. Litig. 219 (1994).

43. *Id.* at 238.

44. *Id.* at 238.

45. *Id.* at 223.

46. *Id.*

47. *Id.* at 241–42.

48. *Id.* at 243.

49. *Id.* at 243–44.

50. *Id.* at 244.

51. *Id.*

52. Justice Ward Hunt (1873), quotations excerpted from J. Kendall Few, *In Defense of Trial by Jury: Vols. I and II* (Greenville, SC: American Jury Trial Foundation, 1993); *Sioux City & Pac. R.R. v. Stout*, 84 U.S. (17 Wall.) 657, 664 (1873).

53. William G. Young, "Vanishing Trials, Vanishing Juries, Vanishing Constitution," 40 Suffolk U. L. Rev. 67, 69 (2006), *quoting* Harry Kalven Jr. & Hans Zeisel, *The American Jury* (Chicago: University of Chicago Press 1966), 499.

54. *United States ex rel. McCann v. Adams*, 126 F. 2d 774, 775–76 (2d Cir.), *rev'd on other grounds*, 317 U.S. 269 (1942).

55. *United States v. Kandirakis*, 441 F. Supp. 2d 282, 315 (D. Mass. 2006).

56. Barkow, "Recharging the Jury," 152 U. Pa. L. Rev. at 121.

57. *Id.* at 62.

58. *See, for example*, *Brown v. Mississippi*, 297 U.S. 298 (1936).

59. Young, "Vanishing Trials," 40 Suffolk U. L. Rev. at 69.

60. William L. Dwyer, *In the Hands of the People: The Trial Jury's Origins, Triumphs, Troubles, and Future in American Democracy* (New York: Thomas Dunne, St. Martin's Press, 2002), 134, *citing* Allen Pusey, "Judges Rule in Favor of Juries," Dallas Morning News (May 7, 2000).

61. *Id.*

TEXT OF UNITED STATES CONSTITUTION

Preamble

We the People of the United States, in Order to form a more perfect Union, establish Justice, insure domestic Tranquility, provide for the common defence, promote the general Welfare, and secure the Blessings of Liberty to ourselves and our Posterity, do ordain and establish this Constitution for the United States of America.

Article. I.

[Section 1.] All legislative Powers herein granted shall be vested in a Congress of the United States, which shall consist of a Senate and House of Representatives.

[Section 2.] The House of Representatives shall be composed of Members chosen every second Year by the People of the several States, and the Electors in each State shall have the Qualifications requisite for Electors of the most numerous Branch of the State Legislature.

No Person shall be a Representative who shall not have attained to the Age of twenty five Years, and been seven Years a Citizen of the United States, and who shall not, when elected, be an Inhabitant of that State in which he shall be chosen.

Representatives and direct Taxes shall be apportioned among the several States which may be included within this Union, according to their respective Numbers, which shall be determined by adding to the whole Number of free Persons, including those bound to Service for a Term of Years, and excluding Indians not taxed, three fifths of all other Persons. The actual Enumeration shall be made within three Years after the first Meeting of the Congress of the United States, and within every subsequent Term of ten Years, in such Manner as they shall by Law direct. The Number of Representatives shall not exceed one for every thirty Thousand, but each State shall have at Least one Representative; and until such enumeration shall be made, the State of New Hampshire shall be entitled to chuse three, Massachusetts eight, Rhode-Island and Providence Plantations one, Connecticut five, New-York six, New Jersey four, Pennsylvania eight, Delaware one, Maryland six, Virginia ten, North Carolina five, South Carolina five, and Georgia three.

When vacancies happen in the Representation from any State, the Executive Authority thereof shall issue Writs of Election to fill such Vacancies.

The House of Representatives shall chuse their Speaker and other Officers; and shall have the sole Power of Impeachment.

[Section 3.] The Senate of the United States shall be composed of two Senators from each State, chosen by the

Legislature thereof, for six Years; and each Senator shall have one Vote.

Immediately after they shall be assembled in Consequence of the first Election, they shall be divided as equally as may be into three Classes. The Seats of the Senators of the first Class shall be vacated at the Expiration of the second Year, of the second Class at the Expiration of the fourth Year, and of the third Class at the Expiration of the sixth Year, so that one third may be chosen every second Year; and if Vacancies happen by Resignation, or otherwise, during the Recess of the Legislature of any State, the Executive thereof may make temporary Appointments until the next Meeting of the Legislature, which shall then fill such Vacancies.

No Person shall be a Senator who shall not have attained to the Age of thirty Years, and been nine Years a Citizen of the United States, and who shall not, when elected, be an Inhabitant of that State for which he shall be chosen.

The Vice President of the United States shall be President of the Senate, but shall have no Vote, unless they be equally divided.

The Senate shall chuse their other Officers, and also a President pro tempore, in the Absence of the Vice President, or when he shall exercise the Office of President of the United States.

The Senate shall have the sole Power to try all Impeachments. When sitting for that Purpose, they shall be on Oath or Affirmation. When the President of the United States is tried, the Chief Justice shall preside: And no Person shall be convicted without the Concurrence of two thirds of the Members present.

Judgment in Cases of Impeachment shall not extend further than to removal from Office, and disqualification to hold and enjoy any Office of honor, Trust or Profit under the United States: but the Party convicted shall nevertheless be liable and subject to Indictment, Trial, Judgment and Punishment, according to Law.

[Section 4.] The Times, Places and Manner of holding Elections for Senators and Representatives, shall be prescribed in each State by the Legislature thereof; but the Congress may at any time by Law make or alter such Regulations, except as to the Places of chusing Senators.

The Congress shall assemble at least once in every Year, and such Meeting shall be on the first Monday in December unless they shall by Law appoint a different Day.

[Section 5.] Each House shall be the Judge of the Elections, Returns and Qualifications of its own Members, and a Majority of each shall constitute a Quorum to do Business; but a smaller Number may adjourn from day to day, and may be authorized to compel the Attendance of absent Members, in such Manner, and under such Penalties as each House may provide.

Each House may determine the Rules of its Proceedings, punish its Members for disorderly Behaviour, and, with the Concurrence of two thirds, expel a Member.

Each House shall keep a Journal of its Proceedings, and from time to time publish the same, excepting such Parts as may in their Judgment require Secrecy; and the

Yeas and Nays of the Members of either House on any question shall, at the Desire of one fifth of those Present, be entered on the Journal.

Neither House, during the Session of Congress, shall, without the Consent of the other, adjourn for more than three days, nor to any other Place than that in which the two Houses shall be sitting.

[Section 6.] The Senators and Representatives shall receive a Compensation for their Services, to be ascertained by Law, and paid out of the Treasury of the United States. They shall in all Cases, except Treason, Felony and Breach of the Peace, be privileged from Arrest during their Attendance at the Session of their respective Houses, and in going to and returning from the same; and for any Speech or Debate in either House, they shall not be questioned in any other Place.

No Senator or Representative shall, during the Time for which he was elected, be appointed to any civil Office under the Authority of the United States, which shall have been created, or the Emoluments whereof shall have been encreased during such time; and no Person holding any Office under the United States, shall be a Member of either House during his Continuance in Office.

[Section 7.] All Bills for raising Revenue shall originate in the House of Representatives; but the Senate may propose or concur with Amendments as on other Bills.

Every Bill which shall have passed the House of Representatives and the Senate, shall, before it become a Law, be presented to the President of the United States; If he approve he shall sign it, but if not he shall return it, with his Objections to that House in which it shall have originated, who shall enter the Objections at large on their Journal, and proceed to reconsider it. If after such Reconsideration two thirds of that House shall agree to pass the Bill, it shall be sent, together with the Objections, to the other House, by which it shall likewise be reconsidered, and if approved by two thirds of that House, it shall become a Law. But in all such Cases the Votes of both Houses shall be determined by yeas and Nays, and the Names of the Persons voting for and against the Bill shall be entered on the Journal of each House respectively. If any Bill shall not be returned by the President within ten Days (Sundays excepted) after it shall have been presented to him, the Same shall be a Law, in like Manner as if he had signed it, unless the Congress by their Adjournment prevent its Return, in which Case it shall not be a Law.

Every Order, Resolution, or Vote to which the Concurrence of the Senate and House of Representatives may be necessary (except on a question of Adjournment) shall be presented to the President of the United States; and before the Same shall take Effect, shall be approved by him, or being disapproved by him, shall be repassed by two thirds of the Senate and House of Representatives, according to the Rules and Limitations prescribed in the Case of a Bill.

[Section 8.] The Congress shall have Power To lay and collect Taxes, Duties, Imposts and Excises, to pay the Debts and provide for the common Defence and general Welfare of the United States; but all Duties, Imposts and Excises shall be uniform throughout the United States;

To borrow Money on the credit of the United States;

To regulate Commerce with foreign Nations, and among the several States, and with the Indian Tribes;

To establish an uniform Rule of Naturalization, and uniform Laws on the subject of Bankruptcies throughout the United States;

To coin Money, regulate the Value thereof, and of foreign Coin, and fix the Standard of Weights and Measures;

To provide for the Punishment of counterfeiting the Securities and current Coin of the United States;

To establish Post Offices and post Roads;

To promote the Progress of Science and useful Arts, by securing for limited Times to Authors and Inventors the exclusive Right to their respective Writings and Discoveries;

To constitute Tribunals inferior to the supreme Court;

To define and punish Piracies and Felonies committed on the high Seas, and Offences against the Law of Nations;

To declare War, grant Letters of Marque and Reprisal, and make Rules concerning Captures on Land and Water;

To raise and support Armies, but no Appropriation of Money to that Use shall be for a longer Term than two Years;

To provide and maintain a Navy;

To make Rules for the Government and Regulation of the land and naval Forces;

To provide for calling forth the Militia to execute the Laws of the Union, suppress Insurrections and repel Invasions;

To provide for organizing, arming, and disciplining, the Militia, and for governing such Part of them as may be employed in the Service of the United States, reserving to the States respectively, the Appointment of the Officers, and the Authority of training the Militia according to the discipline prescribed by Congress;

To exercise exclusive Legislation in all Cases whatsoever, over such District (not exceeding ten Miles square) as may, by Cession of particular States, and the Acceptance of Congress, become the Seat of the Government of the United States, and to exercise like Authority over all Places purchased by the Consent of the Legislature of the State in which the Same shall be, for the Erection of Forts, Magazines, Arsenals, dock-Yards, and other needful Buildings;—And

To make all Laws which shall be necessary and proper for carrying into Execution the foregoing Powers, and all other Powers vested by this Constitution in the Government of the United States, or in any Department or Officer thereof.

[Section 9.] The Migration or Importation of such Persons as any of the States now existing shall think proper to admit, shall not be prohibited by the Congress prior to the Year one thousand eight hundred and eight, but a Tax or duty may be imposed on such Importation, not exceeding ten dollars for each Person.

The Privilege of the Writ of Habeas Corpus shall not be suspended, unless when in Cases of Rebellion or Invasion the public Safety may require it.

No Bill of Attainder or ex post facto Law shall be passed.

No Capitation, or other direct, Tax shall be laid, unless in Proportion to the Census or Enumeration herein before directed to be taken.

No Tax or Duty shall be laid on Articles exported from any State.

No Preference shall be given by any Regulation of Commerce or Revenue to the Ports of one State over those of another; nor shall Vessels bound to, or from, one State, be obliged to enter, clear, or pay Duties in another.

No Money shall be drawn from the Treasury, but in Consequence of Appropriations made by Law; and a regular Statement and Account of the Receipts and Expenditures of all public Money shall be published from time to time.

No Title of Nobility shall be granted by the United States: And no Person holding any Office of Profit or Trust under them, shall, without the Consent of the Congress, accept of any present, Emolument, Office, or Title, of any kind whatever, from any King, Prince, or foreign State.

[Section 10.] No State shall enter into any Treaty, Alliance, or Confederation; grant Letters of Marque and Reprisal; coin Money; emit Bills of Credit; make any

Thing but gold and silver Coin a Tender in Payment of Debts; pass any Bill of Attainder, ex post facto Law, or Law impairing the Obligation of Contracts, or grant any Title of Nobility.

No State shall, without the Consent of the Congress, lay any Imposts or Duties on Imports or Exports, except what may be absolutely necessary for executing it's inspection Laws; and the net Produce of all Duties and Imposts, laid by any State on Imports or Exports, shall be for the Use of the Treasury of the United States; and all such Laws shall be subject to the Revision and Controul of the Congress.

No State shall, without the Consent of Congress, lay any Duty of Tonnage, keep Troops, or Ships of War in time of Peace, enter into any Agreement or Compact with another State, or with a foreign Power, or engage in War, unless actually invaded, or in such imminent Danger as will not admit of delay.

Article. II.

[Section 1.] The executive Power shall be vested in a President of the United States of America. He shall hold his Office during the Term of four Years, and, together with the Vice President, chosen for the same Term, be elected, as follows:

Each State shall appoint, in such Manner as the Legislature thereof may direct, a Number of Electors, equal to the whole Number of Senators and Representatives to which the State may be entitled in the Congress: but no Senator or Representative, or Person holding an Office of Trust or Profit under the United States, shall be appointed an Elector.

The Electors shall meet in their respective States, and vote by Ballot for two Persons, of whom one at least shall not be an Inhabitant of the same State with themselves. And they shall make a List of all the Persons voted for, and of the Number of Votes for each; which List they shall sign and certify, and transmit sealed to the Seat of the Government of the United States, directed to the President of the Senate. The President of the Senate shall, in the Presence of the Senate and House of Representatives, open all the Certificates, and the Votes shall then be counted. The Person having the greatest Number of Votes shall be the President, if such Number be a Majority of the whole Number of Electors appointed; and if there be more than one who have such Majority, and have an equal Number of Votes, then the House of Representatives shall immediately chuse by Ballot one of them for President; and if no Person have a Majority, then from the five highest on the List the said House shall in like Manner chuse the President. But in chusing the President, the Votes shall be taken by States, the Representation from each State having one Vote; a quorum for this Purpose shall consist of a Member or Members from two thirds of the States, and a Majority of all the States shall be necessary to a Choice. In every Case, after the Choice of the President, the Person having the greatest Number of Votes of the Electors shall be the Vice President. But if there should remain two or more who have equal Votes, the Senate shall chuse from them by Ballot the Vice President.

The Congress may determine the Time of chusing the Electors, and the Day on which they shall give their Votes; which Day shall be the same throughout the United States.

No Person except a natural born Citizen, or a Citizen of the United States, at the time of the Adoption of this Constitution, shall be eligible to the Office of President; neither shall any Person be eligible to that Office who shall not have attained to the Age of thirty five Years, and been fourteen Years a Resident within the United States.

In Case of the Removal of the President from Office, or of his Death, Resignation, or Inability to discharge the Powers and Duties of the said Office, the Same shall devolve on the Vice President, and the Congress may by Law provide for the Case of Removal, Death, Resignation or Inability, both of the President and Vice President, declaring what Officer shall then act as President, and such Officer shall act accordingly, until the Disability be removed, or a President shall be elected.

The President shall, at stated Times, receive for his Services, a Compensation, which shall neither be increased nor diminished during the Period for which he shall have been elected, and he shall not receive within that Period any other Emolument from the United States, or any of them.

Before he enter on the Execution of his Office, he shall take the following Oath or Affirmation:—"I do solemnly swear (or affirm) that I will faithfully execute the Office of President of the United States, and will to the best of my Ability, preserve, protect and defend the Constitution of the United States."

[Section 2.] The President shall be Commander in Chief of the Army and Navy of the United States, and of the Militia of the several States, when called into the actual Service of the United States; he may require the

Opinion, in writing, of the principal Officer in each of the executive Departments, upon any Subject relating to the Duties of their respective Offices, and he shall have Power to grant Reprieves and Pardons for Offences against the United States, except in Cases of Impeachment.

He shall have Power, by and with the Advice and Consent of the Senate, to make Treaties, provided two thirds of the Senators present concur; and he shall nominate, and by and with the Advice and Consent of the Senate, shall appoint Ambassadors, other public Ministers and Consuls, Judges of the supreme Court, and all other Officers of the United States, whose Appointments are not herein otherwise provided for, and which shall be established by Law: but the Congress may by Law vest the Appointment of such inferior Officers, as they think proper, in the President alone, in the Courts of Law, or in the Heads of Departments.

The President shall have Power to fill up all Vacancies that may happen during the Recess of the Senate, by granting Commissions which shall expire at the End of their next Session.

[Section 3.] He shall from time to time give to the Congress Information of the State of the Union, and recommend to their Consideration such Measures as he shall judge necessary and expedient; he may, on extraordinary Occasions, convene both Houses, or either of them, and in Case of Disagreement between them, with Respect to the Time of Adjournment, he may adjourn them to such Time as he shall think proper; he shall receive Ambassadors and other public Ministers; he shall take Care that the Laws be faithfully executed, and shall Commission all the Officers of the United States.

[Section 4.] The President, Vice President and all civil Officers of the United States, shall be removed from Office on Impeachment for, and Conviction of, Treason, Bribery, or other high Crimes and Misdemeanors.

Article. III.

[Section 1.] The judicial Power of the United States shall be vested in one supreme Court, and in such inferior Courts as the Congress may from time to time ordain and establish. The Judges, both of the supreme and inferior Courts, shall hold their Offices during good Behaviour, and shall, at stated Times, receive for their Services a Compensation, which shall not be diminished during their Continuance in Office.

[Section 2.] The judicial Power shall extend to all Cases, in Law and Equity, arising under this Constitution, the Laws of the United States, and Treaties made, or which shall be made, under their Authority;—to all Cases affecting Ambassadors, other public Ministers and Consuls;—to all Cases of admiralty and maritime Jurisdiction;—to Controversies to which the United States shall be a Party;—to Controversies between two or more States;—between a State and Citizens of another State;—between Citizens of different States;—between Citizens of the same State claiming Lands under Grants of different States, and between a State, or the Citizens thereof, and foreign States, Citizens or Subjects.

In all Cases affecting Ambassadors, other public Ministers and Consuls, and those in which a State shall be Party, the supreme Court shall have original Jurisdiction. In all the other Cases before mentioned, the supreme Court shall have appellate Jurisdiction, both as to Law and Fact, with such Exceptions, and under such Regulations as the Congress shall make.

The Trial of all Crimes, except in Cases of Impeachment, shall be by Jury; and such Trial shall be held in the State where the said Crimes shall have been committed; but when not committed within any State, the Trial shall be at such Place or Places as the Congress may by Law have directed.

[Section 3.] Treason against the United States shall consist only in levying War against them, or in adhering to their Enemies, giving them Aid and Comfort. No Person shall be convicted of Treason unless on the Testimony of two Witnesses to the same overt Act, or on Confession in open Court.

The Congress shall have Power to declare the Punishment of Treason, but no Attainder of Treason shall work Corruption of Blood, or Forfeiture except during the Life of the Person attainted.

Article. IV.

[Section 1.] Full Faith and Credit shall be given in each State to the public Acts, Records, and judicial Proceedings of every other State. And the Congress may by general Laws prescribe the Manner in which such Acts, Records and Proceedings shall be proved, and the Effect thereof.

[Section 2.] The Citizens of each State shall be entitled to all Privileges and Immunities of Citizens in the several States.

A Person charged in any State with Treason, Felony, or other Crime, who shall flee from Justice, and be found in another State, shall on Demand of the executive Authority of the State from which he fled, be delivered up, to be removed to the State having Jurisdiction of the Crime.

No Person held to Service or Labour in one State, under the Laws thereof, escaping into another, shall, in Consequence of any Law or Regulation therein, be discharged from such Service or Labour, but shall be delivered up on Claim of the Party to whom such Service or Labour may be due.

[Section 3.] New States may be admitted by the Congress into this Union; but no new State shall be formed or erected within the Jurisdiction of any other State; nor any State be formed by the Junction of two or more States, or Parts of States, without the Consent of the Legislatures of the States concerned as well as of the Congress.

The Congress shall have Power to dispose of and make all needful Rules and Regulations respecting the Territory or other Property belonging to the United States; and nothing in this Constitution shall be so construed as to Prejudice any Claims of the United States, or of any particular State.

[Section 4.] The United States shall guarantee to every State in this Union a Republican Form of Government, and shall protect each of them against Invasion; and on Application of the Legislature, or of the Executive (when the Legislature cannot be convened), against domestic Violence.

Article. V.

The Congress, whenever two thirds of both Houses shall deem it necessary, shall propose Amendments to this Constitution, or, on the Application of the Legislatures of two thirds of the several States, shall call a Convention for proposing Amendments, which, in either Case, shall be valid to all Intents and Purposes, as Part of this Constitution, when ratified by the Legislatures of three fourths of the several States, or by Conventions in three fourths thereof, as the one or the other Mode of Ratification may be proposed by the Congress; Provided that no Amendment which may be made prior to the Year One thousand eight hundred and eight shall in any Manner affect the first and fourth Clauses in the Ninth Section of the first Article; and that no State, without its Consent, shall be deprived of its equal Suffrage in the Senate.

Article. VI.

All Debts contracted and Engagements entered into, before the Adoption of this Constitution, shall be as valid against the United States under this Constitution, as under the Confederation.

This Constitution, and the Laws of the United States which shall be made in Pursuance thereof; and all Treaties made, or which shall be made, under the Authority of the United States, shall be the supreme Law of the Land; and the Judges in every State shall be bound thereby, any Thing in the Constitution or Laws of any State to the Contrary notwithstanding.

The Senators and Representatives before mentioned, and the Members of the several State Legislatures, and all executive and judicial Officers, both of the United States and of the several States, shall be bound by Oath or Affirmation, to support this Constitution; but no religious Test shall ever be required as a Qualification to any Office or public Trust under the United States.

Article. VII.

The Ratification of the Conventions of nine States, shall be sufficient for the Establishment of this Constitution between the States so ratifying the Same.

Attest William Jackson
Secretary

done in Convention by the Unanimous Consent of the States present the Seventeenth Day of September in the Year of our Lord one thousand seven hundred and Eighty seven and of the Independence of the United States of America the Twelfth In witness whereof We have hereunto subscribed our Names,

George Washington—President and deputy from Virginia

New Hampshire—John Langdon, Nicholas Gilman

Massachusetts—Nathaniel Gorham, Rufus King

Connecticut—William Samuel Johnson, Roger Sherman

New York—Alexander Hamilton

New Jersey—William Livingston, David Brearley, William Paterson, Jonathan Dayton

Pennsylvania—Benjamin Franklin, Thomas Mifflin, Robert Morris, George Clymer, Thomas Fitzsimons, Jared Ingersoll, James Wilson, Gouvernour Morris

Delaware—George Read, Gunning Bedford Jr., John Dickinson, Richard Bassett, Jacob Broom

Maryland—James McHenry, Daniel of St Thomas Jenifer, Daniel Carroll

Virginia—John Blair, James Madison Jr.

North Carolina—William Blount, Richard Dobbs Spaight, Hugh Williamson

South Carolina—John Rutledge, Charles Cotesworth Pinckney, Charles Pinckney, Pierce Butler

Georgia—William Few, Abraham Baldwin

In Convention Monday, September 17th, 1787.

Present
The States of

New Hampshire, Massachusetts, Connecticut, Mr. Hamilton from New York, New Jersey, Pennsylvania, Delaware, Maryland, Virginia, North Carolina, South Carolina and Georgia.

Resolved,

That the preceeding Constitution be laid before the United States in Congress assembled, and that it is the Opinion of this Convention, that it should afterwards be submitted to a Convention of Delegates, chosen in each State by the People thereof, under the Recommendation of its Legislature, for their Assent and Ratification; and that each Convention assenting to, and ratifying the Same, should give Notice thereof to the United States in Congress assembled. Resolved, That it is the Opinion of this Convention, that as soon as the Conventions of nine States shall have ratified this Constitution, the United States in Congress assembled should fix a Day on which Electors should be appointed by the States which have ratified the same, and a Day on which the Electors should assemble to vote for the President, and the Time and Place for commencing Proceedings under this Constitution. That after such Publication the Electors should be appointed, and the Senators and Representatives elected: That the Electors should meet on the Day fixed for the Election of the President, and should transmit their Votes certified, signed, sealed and directed, as the Constitution requires, to the Secretary of the United States in Congress assembled, that the Senators and Representatives should convene at the Time and Place assigned; that the Senators should appoint a President of the Senate, for the sole purpose of receiving, opening and counting the Votes for President; and, that after he shall be chosen, the Congress, together with the President, should, without Delay, proceed to execute this Constitution.

By the Unanimous Order of the Convention

Go. Washington—Presidt.
W. Jackson Secretary.

Amendment 1

Congress shall make no law respecting an establishment of religion, or prohibiting the free exercise thereof; or abridging the freedom of speech, or of the press; or the right of the people peaceably to assemble, and to petition the Government for a redress of grievances.

Amendment 2

A well regulated Militia, being necessary to the security of a free State, the right of the people to keep and bear Arms, shall not be infringed.

Amendment 3

No Soldier shall, in time of peace be quartered in any house, without the consent of the Owner, nor in time of war, but in a manner to be prescribed by law.

Amendment 4

The right of the people to be secure in their persons, houses, papers, and effects, against unreasonable searches and seizures, shall not be violated, and no Warrants shall issue, but upon probable cause, supported by Oath or affirmation, and particularly describing the place to be searched, and the persons or things to be seized.

Amendment 5

No person shall be held to answer for a capital, or otherwise infamous crime, unless on a presentment or indictment of a Grand Jury, except in cases arising in the land or naval forces, or in the Militia, when in actual service in time of War or public danger; nor shall any person be subject for the same offense to be twice put in jeopardy of life or limb; nor shall be compelled in any criminal case to be a witness against himself, nor be deprived of life, liberty, or property, without due process of law; nor shall private property be taken for public use, without just compensation.

Amendment 6

In all criminal prosecutions, the accused shall enjoy the right to a speedy and public trial, by an impartial jury of the State and district wherein the crime shall have been committed, which district shall have been previously ascertained by law, and to be informed of the nature and cause of the accusation; to be confronted with the witnesses against him; to have compulsory process for obtaining witnesses in his favor, and to have the Assistance of Counsel for his defence.

Amendment 7

In Suits at common law, where the value in controversy shall exceed twenty dollars, the right of trial by jury shall be preserved, and no fact tried by a jury, shall be otherwise re-examined in any Court of the United States, than according to the rules of the common law.

Amendment 8

Excessive bail shall not be required, nor excessive fines imposed, nor cruel and unusual punishments inflicted.

Amendment 9

The enumeration in the Constitution, of certain rights, shall not be construed to deny or disparage others retained by the people.

Amendment 10

The powers not delegated to the United States by the Constitution, nor prohibited by it to the States, are reserved to the States respectively, or to the people.

Amendment 11

The Judicial power of the United States shall not be construed to extend to any suit in law or equity, commenced or prosecuted against one of the United States by

Citizens of another State, or by Citizens or Subjects of any Foreign State.

Amendment 12

The Electors shall meet in their respective states, and vote by ballot for President and Vice-President, one of whom, at least, shall not be an inhabitant of the same state with themselves; they shall name in their ballots the person voted for as President, and in distinct ballots the person voted for as Vice-President, and they shall make distinct lists of all persons voted for as President, and of all persons voted for as Vice-President and of the number of votes for each, which lists they shall sign and certify, and transmit sealed to the seat of the government of the United States, directed to the President of the Senate;

The President of the Senate shall, in the presence of the Senate and House of Representatives, open all the certificates and the votes shall then be counted;

The person having the greatest Number of votes for President, shall be the President, if such number be a majority of the whole number of Electors appointed; and if no person have such majority, then from the persons having the highest numbers not exceeding three on the list of those voted for as President, the House of Representatives shall choose immediately, by ballot, the President. But in choosing the President, the votes shall be taken by states, the representation from each state having one vote; a quorum for this purpose shall consist of a member or members from two-thirds of the states, and a majority of all the states shall be necessary to a choice. And if the House of Representatives shall not choose a President whenever the right of choice shall devolve upon them, before the fourth day of March next following, then the Vice-President shall act as President, as in the case of the death or other constitutional disability of the President.

The person having the greatest number of votes as Vice-President, shall be the Vice-President, if such number be a majority of the whole number of Electors appointed, and if no person have a majority, then from the two highest numbers on the list, the Senate shall choose the Vice-President; a quorum for the purpose shall consist of two-thirds of the whole number of Senators, and a majority of the whole number shall be necessary to a choice. But no person constitutionally ineligible to the office of President shall be eligible to that of Vice-President of the United States.

Amendment 13

1. Neither slavery nor involuntary servitude, except as a punishment for crime whereof the party shall have been duly convicted, shall exist within the United States, or any place subject to their jurisdiction.

2. Congress shall have power to enforce this article by appropriate legislation.

Amendment 14

1. All persons born or naturalized in the United States, and subject to the jurisdiction thereof, are citizens of the United States and of the State wherein they reside. No State shall make or enforce any law which shall abridge the privileges or immunities of citizens of the United States; nor shall any State deprive any person of life, liberty, or property, without due process of law; nor deny to any person within its jurisdiction the equal protection of the laws.

2. Representatives shall be apportioned among the several States according to their respective numbers,

counting the whole number of persons in each State, excluding Indians not taxed. But when the right to vote at any election for the choice of electors for President and Vice-President of the United States, Representatives in Congress, the Executive and Judicial officers of a State, or the members of the Legislature thereof, is denied to any of the male inhabitants of such State, being twenty-one years of age, and citizens of the United States, or in any way abridged, except for participation in rebellion, or other crime, the basis of representation therein shall be reduced in the proportion which the number of such male citizens shall bear to the whole number of male citizens twenty-one years of age in such State.

3. No person shall be a Senator or Representative in Congress, or elector of President and Vice-President, or hold any office, civil or military, under the United States, or under any State, who, having previously taken an oath, as a member of Congress, or as an officer of the United States, or as a member of any State legislature, or as an executive or judicial officer of any State, to support the Constitution of the United States, shall have engaged in insurrection or rebellion against the same, or given aid or comfort to the enemies thereof. But Congress may by a vote of two-thirds of each House, remove such disability.

4. The validity of the public debt of the United States, authorized by law, including debts incurred for payment of pensions and bounties for services in suppressing insurrection or rebellion, shall not be questioned. But neither the United States nor any State shall assume or pay any debt or obligation incurred in aid of insurrection or rebellion against the United States, or any claim for the loss or emancipation of any slave; but all such debts, obligations and claims shall be held illegal and void.

5. The Congress shall have power to enforce, by appropriate legislation, the provisions of this article.

Amendment 15

1. The right of citizens of the United States to vote shall not be denied or abridged by the United States or by any State on account of race, color, or previous condition of servitude.

2. The Congress shall have power to enforce this article by appropriate legislation.

Amendment 16

The Congress shall have power to lay and collect taxes on incomes, from whatever source derived, without apportionment among the several States, and without regard to any census or enumeration.

Amendment 17

The Senate of the United States shall be composed of two Senators from each State, elected by the people thereof, for six years; and each Senator shall have one vote. The electors in each State shall have the qualifications requisite for electors of the most numerous branch of the State legislatures.

When vacancies happen in the representation of any State in the Senate, the executive authority of such State shall issue writs of election to fill such vacancies: Provided, That the legislature of any State may empower the executive thereof to make temporary appointments until the people fill the vacancies by election as the legislature may direct.

This amendment shall not be so construed as to affect the election or term of any Senator chosen before it becomes valid as part of the Constitution.

Amendment 18

1. After one year from the ratification of this article the manufacture, sale, or transportation of intoxicating liquors within, the importation thereof into, or the exportation thereof from the United States and all territory subject to the jurisdiction thereof for beverage purposes is hereby prohibited.

2. The Congress and the several States shall have concurrent power to enforce this article by appropriate legislation.

3. This article shall be inoperative unless it shall have been ratified as an amendment to the Constitution by the legislatures of the several States, as provided in the Constitution, within seven years from the date of the submission hereof to the States by the Congress.

Amendment 19

The right of citizens of the United States to vote shall not be denied or abridged by the United States or by any State on account of sex.

Congress shall have power to enforce this article by appropriate legislation.

Amendment 20

1. The terms of the President and Vice President shall end at noon on the 20th day of January, and the terms of Senators and Representatives at noon on the 3d day of January, of the years in which such terms would have ended if this article had not been ratified; and the terms of their successors shall then begin.

2. The Congress shall assemble at least once in every year, and such meeting shall begin at noon on the 3d day

of January, unless they shall by law appoint a different day.

3. If, at the time fixed for the beginning of the term of the President, the President elect shall have died, the Vice President elect shall become President. If a President shall not have been chosen before the time fixed for the beginning of his term, or if the President elect shall have failed to qualify, then the Vice President elect shall act as President until a President shall have qualified; and the Congress may by law provide for the case wherein neither a President elect nor a Vice President elect shall have qualified, declaring who shall then act as President, or the manner in which one who is to act shall be selected, and such person shall act accordingly until a President or Vice President shall have qualified.

4. The Congress may by law provide for the case of the death of any of the persons from whom the House of Representatives may choose a President whenever the right of choice shall have devolved upon them, and for the case of the death of any of the persons from whom the Senate may choose a Vice President whenever the right of choice shall have devolved upon them.

5. Sections 1 and 2 shall take effect on the 15th day of October following the ratification of this article.

6. This article shall be inoperative unless it shall have been ratified as an amendment to the Constitution by the legislatures of three-fourths of the several States within seven years from the date of its submission.

Amendment 21
1. The eighteenth article of amendment to the Constitution of the United States is hereby repealed.

2. The transportation or importation into any State, Territory, or possession of the United States for delivery or use therein of intoxicating liquors, in violation of the laws thereof, is hereby prohibited.

3. The article shall be inoperative unless it shall have been ratified as an amendment to the Constitution by conventions in the several States, as provided in the Constitution, within seven years from the date of the submission hereof to the States by the Congress.

Amendment 22

1. No person shall be elected to the office of the President more than twice, and no person who has held the office of President, or acted as President, for more than two years of a term to which some other person was elected President shall be elected to the office of the President more than once. But this Article shall not apply to any person holding the office of President, when this Article was proposed by the Congress, and shall not prevent any person who may be holding the office of President, or acting as President, during the term within which this Article becomes operative from holding the office of President or acting as President during the remainder of such term.

2. This article shall be inoperative unless it shall have been ratified as an amendment to the Constitution by the legislatures of three-fourths of the several States within seven years from the date of its submission to the States by the Congress.

Amendment 23

1. The District constituting the seat of Government of the United States shall appoint in such manner as the Congress may direct: A number of electors of President

and Vice President equal to the whole number of Senators and Representatives in Congress to which the District would be entitled if it were a State, but in no event
more than the least populous State; they shall be in addition to those appointed by the States, but they shall be
considered, for the purposes of the election of President
and Vice President, to be electors appointed by a State;
and they shall meet in the District and perform such
duties as provided by the twelfth article of amendment.

2. The Congress shall have power to enforce this article
by appropriate legislation.

Amendment 24

1. The right of citizens of the United States to vote
in any primary or other election for President or Vice
President, for electors for President or Vice President, or
for Senator or Representative in Congress, shall not be
denied or abridged by the United States or any State by
reason of failure to pay any poll tax or other tax.

2. The Congress shall have power to enforce this article
by appropriate legislation.

Amendment 25

1. In case of the removal of the President from office
or of his death or resignation, the Vice President shall
become President.

2. Whenever there is a vacancy in the office of the Vice
President, the President shall nominate a Vice President
who shall take office upon confirmation by a majority
vote of both Houses of Congress.

3. Whenever the President transmits to the President
pro tempore of the Senate and the Speaker of the House
of Representatives his written declaration that he is

unable to discharge the powers and duties of his office, and until he transmits to them a written declaration to the contrary, such powers and duties shall be discharged by the Vice President as Acting President.

4. Whenever the Vice President and a majority of either the principal officers of the executive departments or of such other body as Congress may by law provide, transmit to the President pro tempore of the Senate and the Speaker of the House of Representatives their written declaration that the President is unable to discharge the powers and duties of his office, the Vice President shall immediately assume the powers and duties of the office as Acting President.

Thereafter, when the President transmits to the President pro tempore of the Senate and the Speaker of the House of Representatives his written declaration that no inability exists, he shall resume the powers and duties of his office unless the Vice President and a majority of either the principal officers of the executive department or of such other body as Congress may by law provide, transmit within four days to the President pro tempore of the Senate and the Speaker of the House of Representatives their written declaration that the President is unable to discharge the powers and duties of his office. Thereupon Congress shall decide the issue, assembling within forty eight hours for that purpose if not in session. If the Congress, within twenty one days after receipt of the latter written declaration, or, if Congress is not in session, within twenty one days after Congress is required to assemble, determines by two thirds vote of both Houses that the President is unable to discharge the powers and duties of his office, the Vice President shall continue to discharge the same as Acting President; otherwise, the President shall resume the powers and duties of his office.

Amendment 26

1. The right of citizens of the United States, who are eighteen years of age or older, to vote shall not be denied or abridged by the United States or by any State on account of age.

2. The Congress shall have power to enforce this article by appropriate legislation.

Amendment 27

No law, varying the compensation for the services of the Senators and Representatives, shall take effect, until an election of Representatives shall have intervened.

INDEX

ABOUT THE AUTHOR

Andrew Guthrie Ferguson is Assistant Professor of Law at the David A. Clarke School of Law at the University of the District of Columbia, where he teaches criminal law, criminal procedure, and evidence. He graduated *summa cum laude* from the University of Pennsylvania School of Law. He was awarded the E. Barrett Prettyman Fellowship at Georgetown Law Center's Criminal Justice Clinic, and he was a supervising attorney at the Public Defender Service for the District of Columbia. He is coauthor of *Youth Justice in America* (2005).